Ross Talarico

S P R E A D I N G

DUKE UNIVERSITY PRESS

Durham and London 1995

T H E   W O R D

Poetry

and

the

Survival

of

Community

in

America

© 1995 Duke University Press
All rights reserved
Printed in the United States on acid-free paper ∞
Typeset in Minion by Keystone Typesetting, Inc.
Library of Congress Cataloging-in-Publication Data
appear on the last printed page of this book.

If you would learn to write,
'tis in the street you must learn it . . .
The people, and not the college,
is the writer's home.
—Ralph Waldo Emerson

CONTENTS

ACKNOWLEDGMENTS

F irst, I'd like to thank Rick Packard, my good friend, for his efforts to convince a city government that a poet was worth listening to. Without his belief in literature and his interest in the written word, none of the literary efforts described in this book would have occurred.

I'd like to thank Dan Hall, my editor at Gannett newspapers, for his consistent support in publishing essays and poetry that don't often appear on the pages of newspapers in this country. His interest in ideas gave many people, young and old, a chance to share their voices throughout my years in Rochester.

I'd like to thank the many wonderful staff members of the City of Rochester's Department of Parks and Recreation, who, sometimes against the wishes of their supervisors, embraced poetry and creativity and literacy in order to facilitate the self-expressions of their constituencies. I'd like to thank, too, the City Council of the City of Rochester for its faithful support of the writing program in the face of numerous budget-cut crises.

And finally, if I've given anything of myself over the last few years of encouraging others, or if I've instilled in others a sense of giving by a commitment to a process—writing poetry—that opens up hearts as well as minds, I'd like to thank, most of all, my mother, Regina Bird, for the simple, lifelong lessons of loving that she has always provided.

A few explanations. This book covers a time in my life when my position was quite unique—the only writer-in-residence for an entire city (Rochester, New York)—working under the mayor for city government, creating writing programs and literary events, projects and publications, for residents of all ages, skill levels, and backgrounds. That went on for eight years. I had established myself early in the world of poetry, published widely and becoming, like so many of the poets of my generation, a "university writer." But my life as a poet took on meaning when I left academia and discovered that the language of poetry was the language that sang to common people looking for access to self-expression and self-revelation.

This book is an effort, once and for all, to take poetry out of the hands of elitists and into the working vocabularies of the social arts.

I use the term *deliteracy* several times in this text. The term is the title, in fact, of chapter 3. I coined the term to suggest something corporate and systematic that is going on in our country: the gradual disintegration of society's dependence on language. It may be useful for the reader to know the term before coming across it.

Once in a while, I refer to this book as "a collection." I imagine I do because this is such a collective effort—not one author's point of view, but more of a larger perspective based on the emotional, intellectual, and written responses of many. In addition, many of the individual efforts that appear in this book first appeared in some collective effort: on community center Peg-Boards, on xeroxed sheets, in a city-wide anthology, on the walls of a museum, on TV and radio, in newspapers, on the stage in Chicago, and even in a Russian newspaper!

The book is organized in an unusual way. Each chapter contains three sections: an essay on language that also serves to document the writing program and its creation in Rochester; a vignette that traces my own experiences that led to my compulsion to be a writer; and a "workshop" section which serves as a kind of biographical (as well as autobiographical) coda for each chapter. This last section gives the reader both a view of the more practical applications of my approaches to encouraging writing in others and a wider, more encompassing sense of how an entire community begins to enrich itself through the sharing of language arts. There is, I believe, a delicate structure in this format, one which implies strongly the connection between perspective, personal experience, and community enrichment, hopefully creating a sense of reverberation, experiences repeating themselves despite different environments—a notion essential to this book.

Finally, I think of this book as a kind of entertainment and instruction. It is a reminder to writers, to artists in general, that they must work in new ways to make themselves available to a society in dire need of their sensibilities, techniques, and perspectives. It is, at the same time, an effort to communicate to a culture just how essential our poets and writers are in a world that is mistakenly perceived to be composed of strangers.

Ross Talarico
September 1994

There is a recurring image that haunts me.

Oddly, it's an image of warmth, companionship, and yet it still has a haunting quality . . .

It is evening. It must be autumn because the last bonfire is beginning to flicker, the aroma of burnt leaves rising with the dreamlike smoke under the streetlamp. Saying goodnight to my teenage companions, I hop up the front steps and push open our front door (it is *always* left unlocked).

There are lights burning inside the house as well—not flickering, not faint nor bluish, but steady, adequate, precise. Under them, illuminated: my sister Judy, knees up, snuggled up on the corner of the couch in the living room in her hands, one of the books from the arched book-shelves on either side of the fireplace; and on the other side of the hall-way, as I look beyond the darkened dining room and into the kitchen, my father there sitting at the table, sipping coffee and turning the pages of an Ellery Queen mystery. At the top of the stairs, I hear my mother running her bath, and taking a quick glance into Lonnie's room, my eldest sister, I see her writing something into a diary . . .

In my own room, I touch the cloth scapular that's wound around the bedpost before I lay my head back on the pillow. It's not that I'm religious—my father, in fact, is an atheist; but I am superstitious, re-specting the simplest of routines, like repeating the exact same words to my dog when I close the shed door on her in the cellar each evening, in order, I suspect, to make sure each day remains pretty much the same in my life, because I'm happy.

I'm happy because I know each room in our little house is filled with life. I know within each room there's a private life unfolding, and that each maturing life gives depth to that stronger sense of belonging—a family.

I know now, a quarter of a century later, the importance of that recurrent image. Because we had a sense of ourselves as individuals, we had each other as well. The image haunts me now, I believe, because it is one I cherish—and it is an image (I'm afraid) of the past.

It's a cold February night in Rochester, New York; you can feel the snow crisp under your feet as another cold spell blows in from the wintry Midwest. I've just come from the North Street Recreation Center where I met with a sixteen-year-old black youth named Troy Coffie. He was there to finish a poem he had been working on for the previous three weeks or so. *Roses surround the emptiness I discover . . .* he reads to me, matter-of-factly, as if completely unaware of the line's immediate image and lyric.

He had walked the ten blocks or so over to the recreation center excited by a couple of new lines he had jotted down earlier in the day in a study hall at his high school. I drove him home and made my way here, across the city a bit to a dead-end street called Parkside Drive. It is just five blocks from the street where I grew up thirty years earlier.

Alex answers as he said he would. It is already past nine o'clock, a little later than I'd like it to be. His sister, Yolanda, is sleeping on the couch, and Alex turns the sound down on the TV. His mother, Alex explains, is already upstairs, getting ready for bed. Like many black mothers in the neighborhood, she alone is responsible for Alex and Yolanda, for making a living, keeping a house, and making sure the family avoids the troubles so abundant in the poor tough areas surrounding them. She is doing an excellent job.

Alex and I go into the kitchen, me with my notebook under my arm,

Alex with versions of his poem on the table—along with an old Smith Corona typewriter his mother set up so we could type the finished product. I glance at his poem, read the lines—*I stumble over the hundreds of rocks / in the way of my wishes . . .* —and am pleased that he seems to have put all his images together. He reads the final version through with a beautiful, soft voice that reflects the touch of his fingers upon the notebook paper. We agree it's right, finished—and Alex starts to type it on the typewriter.

But he makes mistakes in the first two lines—and I watch him painfully brush on the white-out and try again. I'm impatient because it's late, I'm tired and I want to go home. "Let me type it," I say to Alex, and he understands and we change seats with one another . . .

Two months earlier I had received a call from a program director at the public library asking if I was working with any young people from the inner city who might want to enter the annual junior literary awards contest. The woman explained that they usually solicited only through the city's high schools, but that she had seen some of the poetry that came out of our recreation programs in features appearing both in the newspaper and on television. She sent me a few applications and I asked a few of the older teenagers if they wanted to prepare some poems and enter the competition. When several said they'd give it a try, we began a process that reminded me how desperately lacking were the channels of communication within a city. Ironically—and more importantly, significantly—my enlightenment centered around the creation and sharing of a piece of literature.

I have always defined poetry a little differently than those around me. As a young poet in America in the sixties and seventies, it was impressed upon me by educators, poets, and especially administrative overseers of undergraduate and graduate writing programs that poetry was a "special" activity produced by "special" people. I was informed—with a strange sense of pride, I should add—that no one read it, no one bought it, and hardly anyone except a few other poets appreciated it in any real sense. This assessment, to my bewilderment, seemed to please most of the poets I knew (especially if they were employed by a university), because it gave them their own private terrain. It also insulated them from public scrutiny: if the common reader did not like, understand, or appreciate a poem, it wasn't the poet's fault, it was the ignorance of the audience that was to blame.

Once I attended a conference where a poet and poetry critic from a well-known Southern poetry journal gave a talk about the impact of a critic upon a poet's readers. I can't remember his point, really, but he spoke with such gravity one might have gotten the impression that one word in his critical column might leave a poet scarred and reeling in a room of remaindered books. Of course the audience that day—as with most poetry conferences—was filled with people who worship editors and critics of poetry magazines, those who want to make that "literary contact," those who want to become part of the "special" club.

I was sitting with Michael Braziller, a publisher from New York City with whom I had given a talk the previous evening as a part of the conference. The more important the critic made himself sound, the more Braziller and I looked at each other. He, as a publisher of quality literature, and myself as a writer of poetry, had earlier expressed our concerns about how few books were sold and how few literary magazines read. But listening to this critic, you'd never guess it.

Finally, we took out our pens and scribbled some figures on the backs of our programs. We tried to determine how many people in America might read *both* the critical column in the guy's poetry journal and the book of poetry he might be criticizing in that review. We came up with a figure: *about fifty people.*

I wanted to put my hand up and offer our estimate to this gentleman in the midst of his talk—he seemed so burdened, so filled with the agonizing responsibility of making or breaking the elaborate careers of our young poets in America. I wanted to put his mind at ease. But I didn't have the heart.

As I said, I've always defined poetry a little differently than those around me. There may be, of course, an elite who own art or who fund the time to contemplate it, but the experience of art belongs to many, because at the moment of that experience what's revealed in everyone is the core of commonality. It is the center of our beings that is awakened by awareness, however brief or whatever the resources we can consciously relate to such awareness.

Beautiful language touches that core. Phrases that remind us of the depth and melody of our voices, images that remind us of our abilities to envision—that magic moment when words and breath merge with the silence of whatever background a man or woman stands against as a part of the world reveals itself for the first time. And it is not a moment reserved for a special few. It is the Grand Access of our modest existence.

In March I received a call from the public library. It was the director who had invited my kids in the street poetry program to enter the junior literary awards contest. She had some good news. One of our kids won one of the three poetry awards—the *only* kid from the entire city proper to win a writing award. It was a poem by a teenager in one of our poetry/basketball programs at one of our recreation centers (the kids write for an hour and then have exclusive use of the basketball court for another hour). I remember the night I collected the final revisions to type up and send in to meet the library deadline: Germone didn't have his, though he said he'd worked on the revisions. He told me he'd left it on top of the refrigerator at his house, and his grandmother had thrown it away by mistake. I brought him over to an empty room off the gym, gave him some paper and a pencil and told him to write down whatever he could remember of it. Here's what Germone Wright put down that night:

FATHER

On the corner of Seward and Jefferson
I met a bum who just might be
my father.
At least he looked like the
man I once knew.
At that moment memories came
to my mind.
I began daydreaming of the times

he'd take me to the park.
We'd go swimming,
and then play tag until I was
all worn out . . .
Suddenly I was back on Jefferson Avenue
and all I saw was the darker shadow
of life.
There were junkies and dope dealers
just standing around, all centered
on the same thing, some dealers, some users.
Then I thought to myself,
which did my father do? He'd left
so sudden I couldn't follow him.
He left when I was eight
and now I'm eighteen.
As I looked up at the sky
I saw only half the moon, looking so dim.
It looked like a lightbulb about to blow.
As I looked down
the ground seemed broken up too,
cracks in the streets, glass all over.
As I looked up once more
to look around,
I could not see my father,
and I thought, there he goes again,
disappearing,
never telling me where he's going.

At the heart of an artistic expression is the need for an individual to seek harmony with his or her environment. Germone's poem serves this notion well. It is about a boy trying to find the human understanding that can connect the environments he describes—that of the soothing past, that of the depressing present of the street corner, and of course the appearance and disappearance of the man who may or may not be the father missing in his life; and, subsequently, the larger void, the need for and lack of male role models in the inner-city environment. The poem leaves us with a sorrow evoked from a predicament, common to all of us. It is, after all, the loss of integration with our environment that creates not only a need, a predicament, or a conflict, but, more importantly, the evocation of an emotion—and that emotion creates the urge for, if nothing else, a means for expression.

But just as there is a harmony within ourselves in the creation of art, there is another harmony, a nurturing relationship between ourselves that is often lacking in our lives. In the last quarter of a century in this country, specialization has provided the sleek efficiency required of technology and profit-making, but it has compromised a sense of perspective, the ability to see not only the whole picture of our society but the relationship between one kind of experience and another. Too often, History remains a stranger to Ethics, Education remains a stranger to Recreation, Politics a stranger to Art, and subsequently Humanity a stranger to Science. Moreover, we become blind to our own social requirements—to discover ways to relate to each other, to open ourselves up, to relate to each other outside a particular vocation, to find the core of commonality that creates understanding and tolerance.

The experience of the poetry contest is a small example of how an art project can bring together several elements of a community. The library was looking to broaden its exposure to the literary experience. Our community center staff was looking for a way to combine recreation with language skills for the betterment of the neighborhood. When I arranged during school hours to come and work with the kids to complete their poetry project during school time, the teachers were elated to have someone from the community concerned about the same tasks in language development. And of course the parents were a little bewildered but appreciative that a city government was actually paying a writer to work with their kids—in the centers, the schools, and their homes—in a language arts program. The fact that our program provided the only award winner from the city proper was simply icing on the cake, though it suggested, in my mind, a kind of equality of imagination and utterance that perhaps did not exist in other subject areas for some of these kids.

The final product, the poem—an artistic expression—was shared and enjoyed by every participant along the way. Certainly this was a small but incidental moment rather than some grand design, but it illuminated a process essential to a population that understands its needs, whether it be the poetry of a single voice, or the harmony of a thousand voices within a concerned community.

M̲ake a list of five familiar objects on one notecard. Any object you see everyday," I explain to the dozen or so kids in a room off the gym at a city recreation center—*window, telephone, doorknob, mirror, flag, pillow,* etc. A couple of minutes later I have them pick up the second notecard I passed out. On this one, I instruct them, five verbs, ordinary action words, physical or mental, that express what you do everyday—*sleep, breathe, study, remember, identify, sing, write* . . . When someone writes *eat, talk,* and *walk,* I make my first objection and tell them that verbs can be interesting—like *chew* and *swallow,* or even *digest* instead of *eat.* I suggest *whisper* or *yell* instead of *talk,* or even *yawn,* going on to describe it as a *silent scream* we all experience.

Already the pencils are making their way across the notecards, and for any writer, not just these youngsters, *that* is the first step. There is, after all, a universal misconception regarding the "art" of writing. Most people think that writers get great ideas and then set out to write them down. Oh, don't we wish it were so! My distinction between a "writer" and a "nonwriter" is easy: writers write, nonwriters don't! The primary object of the writing teacher is to get students to feel comfortable writing, even if they do not know for the moment what they are writing about. It is essential, it seems to me, that they experience the interplay between the word on the page, however spontaneous, and whatever words or ideas begin flashing in the mind. In this case, with these kids, I've cheated a little.

Even before I handed out two notecards to each youth, I had them write at the top of the worksheet, the blank sheet of paper I gave them, two aphorisms: *Vows begin when hope dies* (Leonardo da Vinci), and *The beautiful remains so in ugly surroundings* (Malcolm de Chazal). I discussed each one in terms the kids could relate to—"How many of you *promised* your mother you would stay out of trouble?" And "What if you stole a Picasso from the art museum and hung it over there in the window of Old Man Marvin's grocery store next to the wall of graffiti?" Then, passing out the notecards, I told them to forget the quotes but keep them in the back of their minds.

The writing process is the bridge between curiosity and discovery, between ignorance and awareness—between a physical rendering of one's surroundings and a realization of self. I don't tell these kids that. I make it a little easier connection. In a word game designed to initiate playfulness, spontaneity, and imagination, I ask them to write a poem (no rhymes, no preaching, no clichés) in ten minutes that makes a connection between three of the words on the object list and three on the verb list. "Let each connection suggest something physical to you, and go on to describe what's happening further, surprising yourself as you write. For example, if your words are *window* and *sleep*, perhaps the *window is sleeping*, and if so, *the glass begins to darken*, and when it does, you no longer see the fence and the basketball court out there but a mountaintop and a glacier. And don't forget to introduce yourself into the setting of your poem—you are a part of the image you create. Write first," I add, "think later." And then, just before they are about to begin, I remind them of the aphorisms. *Make a vow,* I encourage them, and remember how *hopeless* you may be if you do. The pencils begin scratching across the paper. The poetry has begun. On one sheet I read: *the mirror whispers my name*. On another: *the road keeps singing*. I do not tell them we'll be looking for one good line, or two, to be used in the next word game. I just tell them to fill up the page and dream.

Zachary Towns is eleven years old. He became a part of our writing group on Friday nights at the North Street Recreation Center to get some time on the basketball court. But after a couple of weeks, he enjoyed the poetry workshops (the prerequisite to basketball on those nights) at least as much as the ball time. He and his brother Jerry show up every Friday night, eager to write. Once I had to track them down in order to get a parent or guardian's signature on a permission slip to go for a field trip to a museum. Their mother gave me a funny look at the door of their inner-city house, later telling me she thought I might have been a policeman or social worker. She had heard of "Ross," and had seen her boys' poetry on the typed handouts I distribute on Friday nights. But apparently Zack and Jerry's demeanor as they mentioned me led her to believe I was just a young kid hanging around the recreation center. The concept of a serious poet engaging youngsters in the creative process is strange to everyone.

That night Zachary employed one of the word games—describing a place, making it physical, feeling a particular emotion change as he sees something take place—and wrote the following poem:

> I see myself holding a basketball trophy
> on a hot summer day among good friends
> at the recreation center.
> It is summer.
> The pavement is hot against my bare feet.
> The sky is as blue as my bike.
> Who am I? Do I see a happy young boy?
> I look out and see teenagers leaning
> on a fence, passing a gun from hand
> to hand, loading it . . .
> It is summer. Someone is going to die.

The city of Rochester, like many cities, has experienced a significant rise in violent crimes over the past few years, and, as in other communities, the mayor appointed a committee to study violence. The committee suggested several "solutions," most significant among them the hiring of forty-eight more policemen. In the same budget with the increment of almost two million dollars for new policemen, the mayor's administration recommends cutting the community's creative writing program, a program whose intent is not to necessarily make writers out of anyone, but to motivate youth, especially in more positive directions—to help them articulate their thoughts about the bewildering world around them, to help them be aware, in Zachary's case, of the mess they are getting into. When Zachary feels good about the warmth of summer and his own accomplishments as he holds his trophy in his poem, he is an ambassador of goodwill, a poet spreading the word. But in the same breath he is issuing his warnings, his plea—*someone is going to die.*

I include Zack's poem in the column I write for the two Gannett newspapers in Rochester, writing about the nature of violence and my belief that often it reflects the lack of legitimate expression in a society. I suggest we spend a little money to provide programs that create in youth a sense of self-esteem, of self-worth, of accomplishment and purpose (Zachary's poem and the article tacked up on the bulletin board at the recreation center). A few days later I receive a nasty note from the new commissioner of Parks and Recreation—my boss! He is angry about me mentioning the fact that kids at recreation centers are packing guns. For a moment the aphorisms written at the top of the page pour through my mind . . . Isn't that just like poetry, I say to myself, making everything so real.

I don't know what makes the autumn leaves fall, caught in the cool Canadian wind at the end of October, an imperceptible curtain of sorts, bringing a faintly perceptible season to a close . . . but I also don't know what makes other leaves hang on so. I help the six senior citizens into the city van. Despite their ages—Sarah McClellan is the oldest (and perhaps the wisest) at eighty-five—they still have a spring in their legs, a strength in their grasp, a deep burning in their eyes. To go to a school and meet with a group of sixth graders pleases them. Life's experience has made them more curious than ever. The fact that they will share their personal histories with kids sixty or seventy years younger pleases them also. They feel, of course, that they know something about life, and to share an experience, to have that oral history written down, published, and distributed, gives their lives an ennobling quality, gives them a distinct identity, an affirmation of being.

Often I arrange to bring together different generations, youth and elderly, to try to identify those universal moments that bind us through empathy and understanding. On this particular morning I have made arrangements to meet in the grade school library for a reason—it has been closed for almost a month! In an incredible decision by the city school district, in order to accommodate a troubled budget, all grade school librarians have been laid off and as a result most of the school libraries have been closed. I walk the senior citizens into the library where about a hundred and fifty fifth and sixth graders await us. I can't believe what I see!

Every bookshelf is covered with black poster paper. I actually gape, unbelievingly, at the black panorama of shelves—an image that brings to mind repressive, totalitarian states, the bonfires and burning pages of Ray Bradbury's *Farenheit 451*. I pass out the copies of the oral history transcriptions, the stories that we will share and discuss in the next hour or so. For a moment, I feel like I'm doing something illegal, expecting someone to burst in and confiscate our literature.

But the morning goes beautifully. The young and the old share each others' stories, the ones written on the handouts and the ones that come out of this sudden, rich dialogue bridging two worlds quite distinct from one another. When Sarah McClellan shares her assessment of what made "country life" valuable for a young girl in rural Alabama on a tenant farm in the early 1900s, the sixth graders listen:

> It was tough work, thinking back
> but that was the life
> of a country girl; the advantage really.
> Course we knew, I mean *knew*
> what we ate, knew it from the ground
> that it came from. And we knew
> what we wore, from the cotton in our hands
> to the corn sack made into a party dress.
> Yes, we knew where everything we needed
> came from. It was our world around us,
> and the hard work was simply
> the respect we gave to our daily bread.

Sarah is asked how much *allowance* she received. She shakes her head and smiles. "Where was it gonna come from?" she asks, adding "There was no money, nothin' . . . but we had fun, and we listened to our folks and worked hard because we knew it had to be done." Two other elderly black women, Cornelia Phelps and Alberta Williams, read their transcribed oral history about doing the wash as a community back in their childhood days in rural Florida:

THE THURSDAY SPECIAL
story by Cornelia Phelps and Alberta Williams
(transcribed and written by Ross Talarico)

On Thursdays, as we got home
from the red schoolhouse, there,
amidst the pines in the churchyard
near Sanford, we'd take off our
school clothes, put on our old clothes,
and, without a thought,
we'd begin the Thursday Special,
cause we knew what we had to do.

The youngest of us would
run into the woods and gather
branches and chips, which we'd toss
into the fire that heated the No. 8 tubs
on the log benches behind the houses.
The oldest children would pump the water
and haul it to the tubs
where the tallest of the kids, usually
the older girls, like me and my
twin sister, Alice, and Josephine and Mamie,
who were tall enough to get our hands
in the tub, scrubbed those clothes clean.

Yes, from Thursday after school
to Saturday noon, everyone would work
together to do the wash.
We all had our chores, all us kids,
from boilin' water to fetchin' the lye soap

from the older folks who made it,
to scrubbin' the clothes, to rinsin'
til the water was clear,
to hangin' the clothes in the warm
Florida air.
We were told once how to do it,
and that was it. It simply had
to be done. It was hard work
but whatever we did, we enjoyed it.

On those hot afternoons,
we'd throw buckets of water at each other,
and I remember the cool laughter
as we rinsed those shirts and overalls
and bedsheets three or four times
til that rinse water was crystal blue clear.
I've never seen anything, in fact,
as white as the shirts and sheets
we washed in those fields, so white
in the southern sun, that the word *white*
could not possibly describe someone's skin.
Yes, we'd sing church songs
as we did our three-day wash;
we'd mimic the priest, and practice preaching
til we got it deep down.
Once in a while we'd steal a chicken,
cook it up, and fan that kitchen
til the smell went away to save us
from a beatin'.

Sometimes the lye soap ate away
at the sores and cuts of our fingers,
but no matter, each of us
carried a bucket, and hauled water
and rubbed those clothes clean
until the rinse water was clear
and our minds were clear,

and til the older folks looked proud
over their children who were learnin'
that hard work and good times
often came in the same breath,
the same moment in fact
there, under the shade of the trees
at noon on Saturday, when the wash was done for the
week,
and we looked at each other, taking
a cool rest, everything so clean
and smellin' so good,
Saturday night just waitin' for us,
feeling the pride and respect
of accomplishment and companionship, together.

One thing becomes clear to me as I see the faces of these students, young and old, express the sympathy and concern vital to the continuum of communities: poetry was never meant to be merely words on a page. Poetry is a way of seeing and appreciating the world around us. It is that particular vision that illuminates both without and within. There is something going on inside the people before me, and the music of a few voices makes believers of all of us: surely each of us someday will find the moment that blends speech with desire. I read to the group another of Sarah's oral histories, a poem about her own education, and I watch the expressions on the students' faces as they try to imagine a grown woman, tired all day from picking crops, taking care of her grandkids, making her way to clandestine meetings at night, life endangered, hoping to get an education:

MY CERTIFICATE IN NEGRO HISTORY
story by Sarah McClellan
(transcribed and written by Ross Talarico)

"You shoulda' been there to see
such a raggedy, hungry bunch,
1400 of us waitin' in the rain and mud
for a bag of yellow meal, lard

and eggs, lines so long
we'd have to camp out, or go back
2 or 3 days . . ."

It was the freedom fighter, Pat,
a sweet girl from Chicago,
who asked me to write that letter
to President Johnson
when we was hungry, and tired
down in Cleveland, Mississippi in '66.
We'd meet at the closed-down
Methodist school for a three-day meetin'
and Pat would give us
some Negro history schoolin', somethin'
which should have been ours
all along. And in the evenin' too,
in our little town, after pickin'
cotton all day, I'd take my
grandchildren, Curtis E. and Linda Pearl,
and we'd meet under the good light
of the moon, and in the deeper light
of our eyes,
there in the churchyard where Pat
would show us photos and read to us
about Negro sisters and brothers
like Harriet Tubman, who done
carried babies on her own back
and drove stubborn women through the hills
at night and into freedom tunnels
of the underground railroad . . .

My letter appeared in the evenin' news,
and with it
a hundred signatures from those
who struggled to write out the proud letters
of their names.

Times were a gettin' tense, oh Lord;
you could feel it in the voice
of the post-master's wife
when I went down to mail a letter
and she'd ask if I knew
where the girl from Chicago, the freedom
fighter was a-stayin'.
The storekeeper would ask too,
and so did the owner of the dry goods store.
It seemed the more we knew
the quieter we were forced to become.

So we hid Pat from night to night in a
different place—stayin' a while
with the minister's wife, but even that
wasn't safe.
Just down the road in Mississippi
we were told of the brush-hopper deaths,
one little colored boy
and two freedom fighters found dead
(and decomposed
under a brush hopper)
in the sprawlin' well-cared yard of a
lady aristocrat who swore
they were the remains of an old horse.
And in Honanah
there was gonna be a march,
and my son, Sammy Lewis, said Mama don't
go—and by the look in his eye
I thought I'm old enough to mind my children,
and sure 'nough,
that's where Meredith was shot.

And one day, someone said, Sarah,
the President sent us
a plane full of food—he got your letter.

So we made our way
to the old school house, and we
watched the county prisoners carry it in
in their grey and white stripes, big as
my three fingers.
Someone said the canned meat was
ground-up cow hearts, but we didn't care,
we were hungry.
We waited in line
for the coffee and yellow meal and grits.
Some judge stood on the steps for a while
and stared us down;
then he sent a young white man
down among us to take photographs of us.
And someone else asked
where Pat, the Yankee freedom fighter was
at . . .

It was just the night before, in fact,
that Pat handed me
my certificate in Negro History,
sayin' what a fine student I had been.
"I don't want to go," she said,
"but my time is up," and then she gave
me a hug.
Holdin' that certificate in my hand and I knew
that a person is a person,
and out of one blood
God created all nations . . .

On our way home, my grandchildren
and me struggled with our food cartons.
The post-master's wife stopped us
and she asked,
"Sarah, by the way, you know where
that white girl is . . . "

I told my grandchildren then, like
I'm tellin' you'all now,
One of these days, you'll run into somethin'
that you'll be quiet about.

And there'll be another day
when all that silence will make you sing.

THE UNDERSTANDING

*A*s teenagers we began to practice our grief. It seems like once a month we would don our awkward black suits, usually bought in the budget section of Robert Hall's, and make our way to Falvo's or Profetta's funeral homes in early evenings.

It was mostly grandparents, uncles and aunts, or distant relatives, a family affair. But once in a while it was one of our own: Bambi, shot through the head while deer hunting; Carl, running his car off a curve one fast night on King's Highway; Larry, hit by a drunk driver as we walked home down Goodman Street after a minor fight at Skinny's.

In some of the funeral home visits I remember thinking that emotion, at least the expression of it, could be induced by repeating faithfully a series of formal gestures. And, in effect, in some ways, that was true. Even with the most remote of relatives, whose names I could hardly recall, tears would inevitably slip down my cheeks as I approached the casket, knelt upon the pew, made the sign of the cross, and glanced at the deceased with whatever compassion a frightened adolescent could muster in the midst of a grief I knew was waiting, surely, somewhere down the line of my own life.

More clearly, I remember a certain giddiness among my friends once we left a wake, even after the death of someone we were close to. We'd sneak off to a garage somewhere and sip some wine one of us had swiped from a pantry at home, and we'd get silly. I remember one fall night after attending the wake of a girl on our street who died of cancer at eighteen, how we lit a pile of leaves and I think it was Mike who tossed a handful of bullets into the fire and we took turns darting past it while haphazardly, directionless, the little explosions rang out a last salute to our dead playmate.

Of course any psychologist could tell you that each awareness of death is really a reminder of the life, however tentative, at the heart of each moment. We had, even then as rambunctious teenagers, some vague notion of mortality; we knew that underneath the bravura, the cocky defiance, we were as vulnerable as the next guy, and that there would be a long series of little deaths to be experienced long before one could close one's eyes forever. The trips to the wake were simply meditations.

Except for one—years before the others—which turned out to be a strange and startling revelation.

I was at the age of reason—seven, I think. All night I kept hearing my aunts and uncles saying "Poor Sam, he's keeping it all inside." Sam was my dad, and all the family and friends were attending the wake of my grandfather, whom I knew well, since he had lived next door. It was a typical, dramatic Italian affair, each relative carrying on with tears, gestures, and disbelief. All except my father, that is—and so they assumed he was simply unable to find a way to express his feelings; and so did we.

Until we got home that evening. My father gathered my two older sisters and me around the kitchen table. He was honest, straightforward. He told us that as saddened as he was about his dad's death, he didn't seem to have any tears welled up inside of him. As a matter of fact, if he felt anything, it was an emptiness inside. Finally, he looked at us and said that he didn't think that he loved his father, nor his mother either, he added, who was still living at the time.

What a startling revelation for us. Imagine! A father telling you during those impressionistic years that loving your parents was optional. What a burden lifted from our little backs. If we were to love our parents (which we would do in great abundance), it wasn't because such love is obligatory, a duty, but because we choose to do so, freely and spiritedly. For some people I've known, the inability to come to some honest terms with the relationships with parents has caused a lifetime of guilt and obsession. I'm thankful my dad tried to spare us all that.

I think back now to those experiences, and give thanks—for those moments during which we were able to distinguish between legitimate grief and disappointment, which is everywhere. It was, of course, a prerequisite to knowing legitimate joy. As a writer, more so as a teacher, I ask myself and others to distinguish between such experiences in order to choose those that are worth exploring through written expression—it's an old lesson: a faithful portrayal of a moment makes us more honest than we ever cared to be.

2. THE DEMOCRACY OF LANGUAGE

On a clear, warm October morning in 1984, I stood in the soft impressionistic light of the atrium in my hometown's city hall. I looked up at the three tiers of nineteenth-century arches supported by marble columns. They are repeated symmetrically in rows on all sides at each level and poised between them are cast-iron goddesses wearing eagle-talon necklaces and plaster-cast lions embellishing the walls. Above me the heads of Neptunes seemed to be on watch as they overlooked the illuminated space where I stood. Such grand architecture suggests a belief in the future, and each new year, at the same time, creates respect for the past. To stand in the midst of it, one begins to understand the nobility of human existence.

Little did I know that the following August, and every August from that time on, the atrium would be filled with young people, senior citizens, blacks and whites and Hispanics together, city council men and women, the mayor, all sharing an annual poetry anthology that contained the writings of Rochesterians who had participated in our community programs.

. . . But at that moment I was in the wrong place. Looking back, it seemed fitting that a poet wandered into such a regal setting, lost and overwhelmed by the columns, marble, and magnificent light that bring to both mind and heart the spirit of Athens. Once, years earlier, I sat in the Theater of Dionysius and had my young wife take a photograph of me, there, where poetry thrived alongside the beautiful monuments that were built in honor of civilized man. I remember feeling a remarkable sense of belonging—not just to a craft, even as I held my poetry notebook in my lap as I posed for the photo—but a belonging to something as grand as a species, one with the unaccountable powers to imagine, envision, and sing. It is no fluke that the Theater of Dionysius is a part of the Acropolis—the theater where poets recited and the first lyrical plays were performed in front of appreciative audiences made up of common people. As a matter of fact, the theater was there first, and the Greeks knew that their dreams of mankind were tied to those who could realize them through the spoken word. Poets, philosophers, and politicians shared the same civic duties—to allow their fellow citizens a glimpse of the human potential for a better world.

What's happened? Where are America's poets? Growing old, stale, and tenured in comfortable universities? Or starving for recognition on the street corners of *deliteracy*? I stood there, alone in the center of the atrium, knowing that in every sense I was in a strange place. But I wasn't sure whether it was the wrong place or the right place. At that moment I had to find a city commissioner's office, and that was in another part of city hall. But as I stood there, perhaps I knew that I could bring poetry to the atrium—that the columns and arches, that the beautiful balconies and, yes, the fig trees that grew there, and the water tumbling in the fountain of the marble pond, that these things represented the poetic spirit of men and women and that the lyrical voices of our citizens were meant to be heard there.

I found the commissioner's office. In the worst scenario, I imagined he would greet me, offer me a seat, wax on in his own lyrical manner about the value of self-expression, and then, on seeing me out of his office and closing the door behind me, break out into such an outrageous fit of laughter that the secretary would rush into his office with a glass of water and a heart pill, and the security guard would grab me, handcuff me, and utter those words that are downright undeniable: *all poetry is inherently subversive.*

But it wasn't that way. Jeffrey Swain, the commissioner of Parks, Recreation and Human Services, had read the two-page letter I had sent him. In it I had described a program for getting kids involved in creative, self-expressive language activities in community centers. I had said this would be a recreational activity that would complement educational endeavors and so forth. Swain is a bright guy, a Dartmouth graduate who serves in Rochester on theater and museum boards—but he is a typical city administrator with budgetary concerns that are often based on quantity of services provided and not always on quality alone, however strong the desire for quality may be. He is, in short, not unlike many commissioners in similar positions across the country, accessible, even to an artist, as long as it is made clear that a proposal is associated with civic consciousness and public work.

However, there are a couple of other factors that might have contributed to the commissioner's consideration of a program for creative self-expression for the community. Relatively new to the Rochester scene (I hadn't lived there in many years), I found out that an old friend owned a bar and restaurant downtown—two blocks, in fact, from city hall. I stopped in to see him one late afternoon and ran into a communications assistant from the mayor's office. Over a couple of beers, I described the program I was about to propose for Rochester. He was immediately interested—not only because he was a writer himself in his job for the city, but because he had studied in graduate school under the poets John Logan and Robert Creeley, and had understood the value of literature and its connection, by more than the Latin root, to *literacy*. He too had a daughter who liked to write poetry (who, four years later, became a part of my city program's Writers' Apprenticeship Program) Furthermore, he knew the commissioner's secretary also had a love for poetry, and indeed, he proceeded to tell her about me and the writing program I'd be proposing. She in turn made sure the commissioner was informed and made the time to read the letter I sent.

It seems that there is an unidentifiable network of people who have an interest in the art of the written word. They are there, everywhere— understanding individually what somehow we can't understand as a corporate body: that individual self-expression is essential to the realization of character. The urge to create may be as innocuous as singing in the shower, or as formal as writing a letter to the editor in a local newspaper. But it is there—not in a few, as we are taught—but in many. It is no wonder that in a country where poetry is usually a publisher's tax-loss write-off and thus doomed to remainderdom, those occasional poets whose work is made available through some marketing quirk that accentuates sentimentality and cliché in the name of literature sell thousands, like the books of Susan Polis Schultz and Rod McKuen. But reading is one thing—perceived, either rightly or wrongly, as a passive experience, like watching TV or listening to music—and writing is another, an active experience where assertion of the individual is immediate and gratifying. Contrary to traditional educational thinking, it's my contention that *writing is the gateway to reading,* rather than the other way around. Furthermore, because it is an active experience, writing in fact is easier for most young people than reading, if the consideration is a meaningful literary experience. In the deep shadows of *deliteracy,* someone has to write on the cave wall before one develops a system to interpret it!

How many times, in fact, has a writer been approached by someone claiming that he or she could write a novel? The thought behind that statement is not simply that each of us has a story to tell, but that given the time and means, each of us could create an assemblage of selected events that would fall together in some unifying pattern, *thus giving identity to an otherwise opaque lifetime.* A novel, in reality, is not just something a writer does, it is a process—selecting events, organizing a plot, aiming for occasional resolutions—that we all long to experience for the sake of our own identity; however, in a culture that does not promote reflective literary arts, it is a process that only a few manage to record with the written word.

Commissioner Swain said, "Okay, let's try it."

And thus began my descent—the appropriate direction for high art in a country that has lost a sense of application regarding aesthetics, even the aesthetics of language. The director said, fine, go ahead. A program director—and this too is not uncommon—felt her own need to develop the cultural and creative area of recreation programs and provided the administrative guidance to get a community-based program in creative writing off the ground. And the descent continued, down, down the ranks until I stood eye to eye with recreation staff who could not believe the city had hired a poet to work with the tough kids at the community centers. Some, of course, laughed and said privately that it was insane to think that these kids would take recreational time to sit down and write poetry! But others agreed, however skeptical, to try it out. I worked, of course, with those with open minds—some of whom, especially the black and Hispanic staff, not only understood the need for the youths' exposure to language development and new role models but seemed to have a less pejorative view, less prejudice toward language arts in general than some of the white middle-class staff. I began the program with a workshop for the entire staff, and gave them a typical word game (literary exercise) that allowed them to write creatively, to actually produce an original poem, in about ten minutes. A few, I could see, were a little surprised at their own abilities.

Still, I continued the essential Descent of the Artist, down to the street corners, to the basketball courts, to the senior citizen centers where a wealth of wisdom and expression lay dormant. I discovered, naturally, what I already knew as a poet: the further down I go, the more universal the language, the more primary the experience. One is reminded too that there is an entire body of language that is expressed there, where the gutteral lyric is as natural as the shrug of shoulders and the furrow of brows. It is all there, and it is as legitimate an environment as any other for a writer.

. . . Still, I am looked at oddly by many. Not simply because I am a poet, but because I express an interest in hearing their thoughts, in seeing their imaginations on paper. I end up having to prove myself. At one recreation center I have to play some one-on-one basketball in order to make my pitch. I hit two jumpers and someone calls me "Bird" (Larry) and the ice is broken. At another center I strike up a deal—every kid I beat at Ping-Pong has to try a word game and write something creative. I beat every kid in the place—even the good ones, and for a moment I feel one of the Greek gods (Apollo, Dionysius?) at my side. Even the senior citizens express a little distrust, but soon discover a writer is a storyteller too, and we share a few episodes, and before long they want to write them down in order to possess them.

My first contract with the city was for six months. The program blossomed in half that time. It is now the fifth year and we have just received a phone call from First Lady Barbara Bush's office, congratulating us on a collection of writings, *Rochester Voices: Uncommon Writings from Common People,* from youth as young as nine years old to senior citizens as old as one hundred and one, to members of our unwed teenage mothers program, to high school basketball stars, to parent-child creations, to stories by the police chief and a city councilwoman, to oral history transcriptions from our elderly citizens, the last of which has given me another dimension of myself as a writer as well. Even the new commissioner of Parks, Recreation and Human Services has a story in the book!

Our lyrical voices, surely a gift to the species, were meant to be heard; our poetic utterances, those instances of human celebration, were meant to be shared. I think back to that critic from the Southern literary review and how without knowing it he was making a pitch for an elitist club in America, and how he seemed unaware or unaffected by the fact that his readership may have been as few as fifty people in America. In contrast, the poetry of the people in the Rochester program, documented in this book, has appeared on the covers of the Sunday newspaper magazines— two hundred and fifty thousand copies on a single day—or featured on our network affiliate television news programs as poetry videos—over one hundred thousand viewers! *So what?* a purist might ask, *what's the difference?*

The answer is perhaps the key to the survival of literary arts in communities throughout America: *about half a million readers!*

Close your eyes. Imagine a room somewhere, a place indoors, out-doors, a specific place where you are sitting or standing or leaning . . . ," I ask the group of about a dozen elderly men and women. They have a blank sheet of paper before them. Some of these people—in their sixties, seventies, and eighties—have written a little on their own, but most have simply told stories about their past experiences in this workshop.

For the moment, they do not write anything. I give them a couple of minutes to envision where they are in their minds—another place, an-other time. When they see themselves clearly in their imaginations, I ask them to respond on the blank sheet of paper before them to the ques-tions I ask. Their responses, I explain, should be spread all over the page, not in any strict linear form, to suggest the random placement of details that exist in the mind. I begin simply—"What season is it?" I allow them a few seconds for their single word response and follow up with "Give me the evidence of that season—how do you know?" And next, "What time of day or night is it? What is it that makes you know the time?"

I follow up with a series of questions that awakens their senses, thus giving each the physical presence essential to the re-creation of a mo-ment: "You touch something—what is it you touch? There is a noise—what is it? There is something moving in the distance . . ." and so forth. I include questions that utilize remembrance and flashback: "You think of another place from sometime past—describe it in a phrase," and "A name comes to your mind—what name?" I include a few questions that anticipate the aspects of tone—"Write down a color, any color"—and questions that simply provide for the connective tissues of this lingual inquiry: "Write down a verb, any verb," "You touch yourself . . . ," and so forth.

Before long there is not only a memory coming to life, there is before each person a page of resources with which one can begin to re-create an experience with words. Florence Frantz, eighty-six years old, writes down these phrases: *a strip of clouds reaching from the orchid sky to the Gulf of Mexico . . . my son Ken coughing . . . Easter lilies and a choir . . . a cantata . . . a privileged view.* In the weeks to come she would write and revise a poem about visiting her son in his home in Florida. Months later we would learn that her son died of AIDS, and she would revise her poem again, the same images finding their way to the proper context of her love and memories. And at our annual reading in the Atrium at City Hall, Florence, on her way there, falls from the steps of the bus. She asks strangers to help her to City Hall two blocks away. I see her sitting at the event I am hosting, and the word is that she has fallen and is ailing. Her only request: that she be allowed to read her poem, which has been published in the new city anthology of writings that we are celebrating that day. Before the standing-room-only midday audience composed of young, elderly, black, white, Hispanic, parents, sons and daughters, grandchildren, neighbors, city council members and the mayor, Florence makes her way to the podium between the arms of the commissioner and me. She reads her poem from the book. We help her back to her seat, from which, after the reception, an ambulance crew will place her on a stretcher and bring her to a hospital because she has broken her hip. She will recover, and during her first week up and around she makes it back, with a walker, to the creative writing class.

I receive a call from one of our assistant recreation directors, Josephine Parker. She is working with a group of elderly black women in a weekly crafts program in one of the city's senior citizen housing projects. Josephine knows about the popular writing workshops for senior citizens and has been reading some of the stories and poems as they appear in the city's Gannett newspapers and has seen them as poetry videos on our NBC affiliate's television news programs. She asks what seems like an odd question: "Can folks who can't write be a part of the creative writing program?"

Perhaps, in my twisted, cynical mind, since I've known heads of freshman English programs and assistant chairs of English departments who in my opinion couldn't write to save the unpublished thesis of their souls, I don't dismiss the possibility. As a matter of fact, hearing the assistant director's description of the group that wants to meet with me and tell their stories ("migrant workers, family people, women who lived on hard work and faith alone, and those who've seen the brutal side of living"), the idea seems not only intriguing, but sensible as well. And on the following Wednesday afternoon, without knowing it, I begin the Oral History Transcription program, which will become one of the most popular segments of the community writing program.

The point I want to make on the pages of this book and that I've strived to make during the past several years of my life is this: like any other professional seeking a purpose in society, a writer must discover and define his or her role as someone who provides a service to the community. There was a time when writers could assume their role, given the nature of our culture—when literature was a mainstay of societal enrichment. But now such intellectual activity remains at the periphery of our cultural experience, and artists must remind themselves in very real terms just how essential they are. They must work to make themselves available. These elderly black women became a wonderful reminder to me. Here was a group of loving, giving, fascinating women with a wealth of stories to share. Their humanity, arising out of lives of hardship, was at the core of the experiences they began to communicate—reflecting the nature of my literary interest in transcribing their words. We gathered weekly in groups, focusing in on an individual's recollection, probing for details, urging each member to dwell deeper into memory. Earnest Radcliffe told me he'd meet me in private, because his story brought tears to his eyes, and "it wasn't right for a grown man to cry in front of others." Mattie Whitley called me a couple of times at home to make sure I had details she could not utter to the group. Harry Nolsch brought in photos from his native South Dakota to "illustrate" his story.

I listened. I asked questions. I took notes, and eventually I worked out the poetic transcriptions of their stories. It became obvious early on that these oral histories turned into literature were popular and important to all kinds of readers once they were published—on the Gannett newspaper editorial pages (which required they be rewritten as prose!), as cover story features of the Gannett Sunday Magazine, in television news features and poetry videos (CBS and NBC), in an anthology of working women's writing from Rutgers University Press, in translations of them in Rochester's sister city Novrogod in the Soviet Union, in Associated Press and National Public Radio features, in my own book *Hearts and Times: The Literature of Memory,* and as the basis of plays by theatre groups in Michigan and Illinois in 1994.

For me, it provided a classic example of how the writer—especially the poet—can provide an essential service to a community. In turn, the writer becomes less a mysterious, eccentric figure, and more a respected component of a process that reveals directly the character of those around him.

TRAIN RIDE
story by Mattie Whitley
(transcribed and written by Ross Talarico)

I. Atlanta to Wyoming

Choo, choo, clickety hiss . . .
I'm on a train, headin' west.

He's a soldier in Wyoming,
and he sounds as lonely as me.
I read through another of his letters
as the train thumps on.
Chattanooga, Sewanee, Clarksville, Paducah . . .
the porter calls out.
I keep his photo at my side,

lookin' so tall in his uniform;
I wonder what he'll think of me?

His name is Tommy Ross,
and I found him listed in
the *Pittsburg Courier,* a colored paper
we get in Atlanta.
I just picked his name and wrote,
and he wrote back.
Six months of letters and then
the invitation to the base in Wyoming.
I took two weeks from the work I do,
cook and nursemaid
and lately what seems just a sentimental fool.
Jonesboro, Red Bud, East St. Lou . . .

In the bag I packed
I carry two dresses, always do,
one black, just in case,
and another the prettiest, prettiest blue.
I carry a Bible,
and read myself to hope and sleep.
The porter brings some hot tea,
no coloreds in the dining car.
But there are stars galore in the western skies,
and I pick one out and
give it a wish, like everyone else
travelin' so far.
I wonder what he'll think of me.

II. Laramie, Wyoming

Kansas City, Atchison, Broadwater, Cheyenne . . .
I'm coming just as fast, and just
as slow as I can.
Choo, choo, clickety hiss . . .
I'm on this train and headin' west.

. . . Before I knew it, there he is.
On the platform, so handsome, and even
taller than his picture,
takin' my bag, my arm, and I'm
still wonderin' what he thinks of me.
At the barracks he drops off my things
and shows me my letters in a duffle bag.
At the café in the servicemen's club
I meet a hundred soldiers
and they all call me Mattie, like they've
known me all the while.

Turns out Tommy Ross, he's got
everything arranged—time off, an apartment
on base for the two of us,
a dance arranged that night at
the servicemen's club,
and after a night of holdin' me
in his strong arms,
an invitation to marry him that week.

"You jokin'?" I say,
and he just nods his head, and then
I nod mine.
The high altitude gives me a headache,
and I think it's never gonna leave,
even as the chaplain is askin'
whether I do or whether I dare;
and when I'm kissin' Tommy Ross
and later dancin' in his arms in my blue dress,
and seein' the soldiers actin' so crazy
toastin' us so on that joyful night,
the headache stays, like a nagging memory,
and all the happiness in the world
can't shake it.

When the two weeks is over
he takes me back to the depot.
I watch him wave from the platform
and I close my eyes for a longer goodbye.
Already the porter is callin' out
his song of destinations,
Northport, Grand Island, Boonville, St. Lou . . .
Choo, choo, clickety hiss . . .
I'm on this train, headin' east.
We said soon we'd be together,
but it wouldn't turn out that way.
Marion, Nashville, Chattanoo . . .
In Tennessee my head got better,
but not my heart.
I read through a batch of letters, and I
looked at the photo that now would never do.
Choo, choo, clickety hiss . . .
I closed my eyes and remembered his kiss.
I was a married woman, and yet,
how could it be:
I still kept wonderin' what he thought of me.

III. Germany, Ft. Worth, Texas, and Atlanta

Six months later, without us ever
visitin' again, he was sent to Germany.
The letters were slow, so slow,
I'd pray . . .
There was so much, so little to say.
I was a married woman,
but no man around.
I was a cook and a nursemaid
and a sentimental fool. Again the photo
was all I had; even Wyoming
seemed like a cool mountain dream.
For two years I waited

for some kind of news, my heart full,
the headache nagging with its memory.
And before I knew it, the war all over,
I got a letter from Oklahoma, and Tommy Ross
sayin' he was bein' discharged, that he
was goin' home, and to get on that train
and meet him in Forth Worth in Texas.

Choo, choo, clickety hiss . . .
I'm on a train again, headin' west.
Two bags this time,
and just in case, two dresses,
one black, the other the prettiest of blues.
Tuscaloosa, Biloxi, New Orleans, Port Arthur . . .
I really didn't know what to do,
apart so long, three years older,
all that loneliness behind us.
I was still a-wonderin' what he thought of me.

And we were happy for a month or two.
Conceived a child in fact,
but it must've been bad blood, because
one night it began to flow,
and I guess it emptied both of us,
and another night Tommy Ross didn't come home.
And then another. And then one more.
I could already hear the porter
callin' out in my mind: *Galveston, Baton Rouge . . .*

And sure enough, a month later
I was standin' on the platform
at the depot in Ft. Worth, the sky
so dark and heavy,
but me in my dress, the loneliest of blues.

And on the train he sat with me awhile,
before the blast of the whistle

and the choo choo and the clickety hiss
of this old train headin' back east.
He said he didn't need nothin',
and then he cried.
He told the porter to take care of me
'cause I had just miscarried and was
short of strength.
When he left he stopped on the platform
as the train began to move.
He waved like he did in Wyoming.
And I closed my eyes the same way . . .
Mobile, Georgianna, Tallapoosa, Atlanta.

It's all a long journey, the one
that leads home.
I carried a Bible, two dresses, a photo . . .
I carried my love, whatever the pain,
and when the porter says *Heaven,* and
gives me his hand,
I'll shake my head kindly, and tell him not yet,
and I'll head on to Atlanta, where
the sun starts to rise,
where the light falls so briefly, oh Lord,
and forms your beautiful tears in my eyes.

MOUNT RUSHMORE
story by Harry Nollsch
(transcribed and written by Ross Talarico)

I can't begin to tell you
how strange it is
to see a face emerge, one feature
at a time, from a distance
only a young boy knows,
there in South Dakota in the Thirties,
among the stretches of cropland,

tied to the river of time
by the brown waters
of the irrigation ditch and good friends.

As an old man now
I go back, visiting George, the
other half of the graduating class
of 1933 at the little country school
we attended in the Western plains.
He now lives in the place
my folks occupied when I left for
the service in 1942.
He takes me into the tiny room
between the ice shed and the house
where I slept as a kid, and he
points to a dusty shelf, one I remember
building over my bed more than
fifty years ago.
Still visible, the two hearts I
carved there, one with an *H,* the other
with an *E . . .*

I think back to Skyline Drive
overlooking Rapid City
below me and the girl next to me
in a '36 Plymouth; the lights seem to
reach for miles. Even the glow
of Ellsworth Air Force Base offers
its promise of a country waiting.
I look up north to the darkness
surrounding Mount Rushmore, thinking
maybe the eyes of those four great men
close at night, like ours,
and maybe they too dream, like we do,
of a vast country filled with
adventure and love . . .

George tells me the young girl
in my mind is now a great-grandmother
living in a town some thirty miles away.
I wonder what we might say
to each other, what anyone says really,
after all these years.
I remind George of the irrigation ditch,
which would bring water to
the fields of sugar beets, corn, and
cucumbers, and where we'd go
on those September evenings for a
"Last swim" of the season, the moon
rising from behind the willow trees
as we rode our horses
out over the Dakota plains.
The moonlight would dance on the
little waves and miniature whirlpools
in the dark brown water of the ditch,
as we'd strip off our clothes
and jump into the ditch, incredibly happy.

I don't know, in fact,
how my father managed those days;
our farm was "dry," we had to rely on
natural rainfall, my father forced
to mortgage his livestock or farm machinery
to tide us over until another harvest.
How he ever fed us during
these times I'll never know. As a
matter of fact, gas always being
in short supply, we only made it once
to Mount Rushmore, seeing the faces
of Washington and Jefferson, and the
half-completed face of Roosevelt
slowly emerging in the midst

of such a barren and beautiful America.
Lincoln's face, his stern resolve,
was still a dream in the stone carver's
strong hands. From that day on
I took some time to stare out
across the miles at those four great men,
and to meditate on my own achievements.

I run my weathered hand, still sensitive
to the touch, over the initialed hearts
in my old room, hardly big enough,
I reflect, for a wish or two, let alone
the contemplation of a lifetime.
I know I'll never make it out to the ditch
again, and feel the cool, life-giving
water under the moonlight.
But no matter where I stand, half
of me in South Dakota, half in memory,
I'm under the gaze of those
four men atop Mount Rushmore,
and I'll think about my own contribution
to a life of hard work, decency,
minor but wonderful adventures,
and of course whatever romance one can find.
And I'll stand back, the confidence
only an old man knows, feeling
that old September wind after a last swim
as we rode our tired horses back home,
that cold autumn wind, like
a sculptor's hands,
forming the expression on my face.

*B*etween us, Kenny and I had seven hits, and winning against an aging
Al's Green Tavern was especially satisfying as we drove home from Edger-
ton Park on a warm Sunday afternoon.

For years Kenny and I were never allowed on the same team. We were
the best ballplayers in the neighborhood, and every time we chose teams it
was understood that he had to be on one team and I had to be on the other.
So as Kenny drove his father's Nash Rambler over the Bausch bridge near
Bausch & Lomb's, we replayed the game with our teenage embellishments,
happy to share for a change the joys of winning together.

Kenny took a shortcut through a side street between Clinton and Joseph
avenues, and when a gang of young black kids looked at us with a strange
hard look in their eyes, we remembered suddenly not only what had
transpired the night before but that we were not in the most amicable place
in town.

"Jesus, don't stop," I said to Kenny, and he instinctively grabbed the bat
from the seat and placed it in my lap . . .

On Bay Street, the previous night, the front porches looked like a mili-

tary fort. Kenny, Frankie, and I walked up Bay toward Goodman, and stopped at several houses to examine the arsenals. Old Mr. DeCarlo held two rusted Winchester rifles, one in each hand, as he rocked away in a granny rocker on his porch, his wife next to him sewing what looked like a communion shawl, with a .38-caliber pistol in her lap. Their dim-witted son, Phil, who was about thirty I'd guess, and who could make tremendous noises by yelling into his fleshy hands, swung a crow bar in the front yard, muttering "nigger, nigger, nigger . . . " all the while.

Al Viola sat in his half-built dragster with two Smith & Wesson pistols stashed in his thick black leather belt. Ray Monterro, wearing some old army fatigues, was polishing a Remington rifle, and his three-year-old son, little Tony, was waving a plastic machine gun in the air.

"Listen to that," said Ray, tilting his head toward Central Park, "the natives are restless." Then he loaded his rifle and placed his eye against the sight in the same direction. "Let those muthas come down here one time, just let 'em . . . "

It was the summer of 1964. Hot times in the city, as the song goes. It was the first major urban riot, and the sirens and gunshots echoed into our neighborhood because it was all going on just a few blocks away. Being tough Italians—well, that along with the fact that we were only on the next higher rung of the socioeconomic ladder—the whole neighborhood became territorial. Dino and Carm and the older boys cruised Goodman Street, guns and tire irons tucked in their laps, self-proclaimed lookouts. A few years later some of the guys would be making their way through the brush in Vietnam.

My father, I realized, was always a little different from the other fathers in the neighborhood. He often took time to think about matters. At our dinner table each night, he'd bring up some idea, like euthanasia, or the existence of heaven and hell, or God for that matter, and would actually ask us for our thoughts. And it wasn't just our family. Many times I'd come home to find a friend, Frankie or Johnny, and once even the street punk, Eddie Fingers, sitting on the front steps just talking quietly.

So on the first night of the riot he asked my sisters and me why the Negroes were setting their own neighborhood on fire. Then he told us that there was an anger deep in all of us, though this surprised us because my father seemed so mellow. He said he felt frustrations intense enough at times to throw a rock through a window. He went on to say that in a world that promises so much and offers so little to a particular group, it was a wonder riots didn't occur more frequently. He then relayed his own story about having to get a scholarship simply to attend high school, and finally having to quit altogether, and how he'd always wanted to get an education and become a lawyer, and that it wasn't much fun working in a shoe factory all his life. And, he added finally, how if he'd have to live in a rattrap and be without a car to get away for Sunday afternoon drives, he just might put a match to his surroundings as well.

He told us, though, not to do the easy thing and just lash out in anger, but to try to understand the reasons that cause people to do what they do. He told us that sympathy, not aggression, was the key to harmonious times, and in his mind the answer was interracial marriage and a race of bronze-skinned Americans.

I made the mistake of mentioning a couple of these thoughts to the guys at Jack's corner gas station that night the arsenal was on display on Bay Street. Was I expecting a running dialogue? I was called "nigger-lover," "black-ass kisser," and of course worse. I was invited to go back to Africa

with the rest of the natives. "Why don't you just walk your ass down to Scio
Street right now and put out your little white hand and tell them you're a
friend," mocked Dino, holding his middle finger in the air, "and just see if
one of those goody goody niggers don't just slice your throat open with the
broken edge of a whiskey bottle . . . "

Everybody laughed and called me names, even my buddies Kenny and
Frankie. But, I understood, they had their reputations to protect; I knew by
their eyes that their mockery didn't come from their hearts.

. . . Just as we approached Joseph Avenue, Kenny and I saw street barricades and the flashing red lights of several state police cars. A couple of
troopers motioned for us to pull over. Apparently we had accidentally
ended up in a restricted area, an area where there had been a lot of damage
done the night before. When the trooper pulled me out of the car, he
grabbed the bat out of my hand, scowled at me and tossed our best bat, the
one with which we had scattered seven hits between us, into his car (we'd
never see it again). Then they stood Kenny and me up against a building
on Joseph Avenue, our hands against the brick wall, our feet spread, our
green-and-yellow Laura's 1889 Grill baseball jerseys and our Yankee grey
baseball pants hardly a respectable set of all-American promotional gar-
ments. One trooper, who was the tallest man I had ever laid eyes on, took a
nightstick and tapped us, with much more force than he had to, against
our shoulders, ribs, and thighs. I turned my head toward Kenny and he
looked at me. Two minutes earlier we had been so engrossed with the joys
of America's favorite pastime we forgot where we were.

Now the situation seemed ridiculous. Two baseball players being frisked
in the midst of a few dozen black onlookers. I looked around. There was a

black woman holding a baby on the other side of a barricade. I saw in her eyes the same fear I felt within. In an elderly black man's eyes I saw the years of frustration that my father had talked about. There was a young man next to him, about my age, wearing a torn T-shirt with a large stained bandage across his forehead. As our eyes met, I saw him yell out to the troopers, "Leave the man alone, they just ballplayers man . . . "

I had the distinct feeling at the moment, and I'll never forget it, that the barricades were not for our safety as much as they were meant simply to keep us apart, to keep us from understanding each other. The troopers flung us toward our car and told us to move our asses out of there and not to come back. As Kenny drove off toward our neighborhood, I looked back at the state troopers dispersing the crowd that had gathered.

I wanted to go home and tell my father what the feeling was like, being frisked by the police and looking into the eyes of the strangers around us. But we stopped at the gas station for a while and, as with so many fleeting moments, I never did find the right words to do so.

Who owns the language?

I have seen all kinds of people visibly angered and frightened when their possessions are threatened. Confronted with losing a home or a car, or even a favorite piece of clothing, men and women quickly turn themselves into activists—doing what they must do to keep possession of what's rightfully theirs. The same holds true when certain intangibles are threatened in the same manner—such as pride or integrity; people hold onto these things no matter what the cost or hardship. But *language* does not seem to be high on America's list of valuable possessions, and as it keeps slipping away from us, as it becomes less and less a force of communication skill to us, someone will profit on our loss.

The fact that over sixty million American adults lack basic literary skills in a country with the most accessible public education system in the world spells trouble. But—*and this is a concept Americans have an incredibly difficult time grasping—it's symptomatic of a cultural disease more than a failure of education!*

There's a word I've been using in the previous pages of this book: *deliteracy.* It is the word I've coined to describe a tragic trend spreading through this country: the gradual disintegration of society's dependence on language. Ask yourself how many people in this country can write their names and a complete sentence and fill out a job application—but cannot read a paragraph and grasp a single prevailing idea, or make a judgment about the value of a single commentary. How many of these people, in turn, cannot articulate their own simple ideas with either the written or spoken word? No one can provide numbers, although studies in comprehension seem to bear out my suspicions—I don't think I'd be far off if I said half of the American population.

Still, when Americans watch TV or read the evening newspaper, and receive the continual bad news of literary and literacy test scores (reading and writing skills), we point the finger at our schools and educators. Ironically, such a short-sighted response is symptomatic of the disease itself.

The cultural environment of our young is not the noise or quiet found between the four walls of a classroom. Cultural environment is, rather, the background against which an educational system attempts its recital. Perhaps it's our misguided notion of the age of specialization that distorts our view, but I'm convinced most Americans fail to understand the essential relationship between the everyday routine of our citizenry and the basic abilities of our young.

Let me be specific. Writing and reading skills are not skills that can be learned through a programmed series of technical instruction. Language awareness is quite different from becoming efficient in basket-weaving, mathematics, jumping rope, geography, or computer programming. Becoming literate is a process of immersion—a baptism in which the whole body is dipped into the waters of language. And it is not simply words to which we expose ourselves. It is the silences around words—*the silences of reflection, focus, curiosity, imagination, concentration*—that form the essential background against which we can express, whether spoken or written, the occasional utterance. These are, of course, the lessons of poetry and the territory of poets.

The truth is that culturally, socially, we no longer provide the prerequisites for language development. Immediate gratification, once a phrase to measure immaturity, is now the norm at the heart of consumerism; it correlates directly with the general shortening of the attention span. In entertainment, sensationalism outweighs insight-producing drama, and the popularity of rock videos, movies like *Rambo,* and game shows serves as a barometer of sensibilities. TV programming is probably the most blatant example of a nation obsessed with one-liners, instant problem-solving, and car-crashing, bullet-blasting resolutions to the human predicament.

Strikingly absent in our culture is any overt encouragement or any inducement to engage the public in some thought-provoking, self-reflective activity. Newspapers, the only daily exposure to the written word for many Americans, usually offer a single page or two of editorials to stimulate ideas and communication. Human-interest features usually end up cute or stereotypical. Fiction—that is, stories that illuminate the human condition and spirit—is almost nonexistent in our most accessible reading inventories.

How few stimuli, really, to encourage dialogue between family members, friends, or neighbors. No wonder the single greatest difficulty with our young is developing the "skill" of listening! Even a walk in the woods isn't complete these days without a Walkman radio to keep one from articulating (or even forming) one's thoughts.

Deliteracy indicates a general lack of interest in self-expression through language and indeed a disinterest in forming perspectives. How does it come about? *It comes from the successful misuse of language!* The culture rewards those who use language to deceive others, and abandons those who use it in attempts to enlighten.

Most of the emotionally expressive language we encounter is commercial—in advertising, pop music, soaps and sitcoms, or brief news summaries. Predictably, oversimplification, cliché, sensationalism, and fantasy are the common elements of commercialism. Those elements may win over converts, but never human intuition. For however inarticulate or illiterate we may be, we are not stupid. Down deep, *where we know things*, we are breeding a contempt for language. Down deep, Americans realize that human awareness does not come from jingles, catchphrases, and summarizations.

But there is, already, a fine line.

In the spring of 1989, I was asked to give a series of workshops and lectures at a high school in Geneva, New York. I was happy to see that the school was employing the state's Artist-Residency Program, a popular and effective program during the seventies, which brought poets and writers to classrooms not only in New York State but throughout the country. In the eighties, these programs practically disappeared—not simply because of budget cuts, but because of budget cuts based on the concept that language development through creative self-expression is no longer a priority. Such a view on the part of education administrators is another symptom of *deliteracy*. I've always been proud to have been a part of the first Poet-in-Residence Program (the former title of Artist-Residency Programs for writers) in New York State outside New York City back in 1970 in Syracuse. I also helped initiate writer-residency programs in North Carolina, South Carolina, Connecticut, Virginia, and Illinois. Being a proponent of such programs, and being sadly disillusioned by their general disappearance in the eighties in America, I was happy to be doing a residency program almost two decades later.

One afternoon in Geneva I was giving a reading from one of my books, a collection of short stories about growing up in the sixties. I read a story called "America's Pastime," the story that appears at the end of the previous chapter. There must have been about three hundred students in the auditorium. They were attentive enough, and seemed to enjoy a couple of poems and another vignette I had read earlier. But about halfway through "America's Pastime," I noticed some unrest among a group of black students to the left in the audience. The unrest continued until I finished the story.

I had completed my reading with that piece and opened it up to questions. A hand went up, slowly, in the midst of the group of black students. It was one of their teachers, and he seemed a bit uncomfortable as he spoke. He asked in a friendly, inquisitive manner, if I could explain the theme of the vignette—and then added, obviously voicing the concerns of the black students around him, if it were a "racist story."

I began my explanation before it dawned on me what had happened. I said sure, it's a story about white racism during the Rochester riots in 1964. I went on to explain that it was about a young boy's initiation into the angry, violent world of racism, and the difficulties he encountered in trying to understand his father's tolerance in an environment filled with fear, hatred, and prejudice. It was a story about racism, I continued, but the point of view is one of antiracism, trying to see racism for what it was in 1964. I pointed out that the most humane understanding of that particular situation came from the young black man who told the state police to leave the young white kids alone, that they were "just ballplayers man."

As I was saying this, it hit me. The group of black students were not listening to the story—they either lacked interest or the skills to do so. All they heard were the words of the dialogue that I'd used to expose the racist feelings rampant at that time—"nigger-lover, black-ass kisser," etc. And without a context into which they could put these words, the words became simply *code words* to alert them to racism; and thus whatever the nature of the story, they could only view both it and the author as racist.

Now this may have come as a surprise to me, but then when it comes to knowing how people react to language, writers may know less than marketing strategists who can put such a listening deficiency to profitable use.

This point, as devastating as it is, is simple: without the ability to perform basic communication skills (reading, writing, *and listening*), we will be completely vulnerable to anyone with a few marketing skills. These corporate marketers already know the power of code words, jinglism, and the avoidance of context as far as making us feel one way or the other instantaneously—the way the kids in the audience reacted upon hearing a single word and being unable to distinguish between racism and antiracism; unable to tell the difference between a sympathetic author and an unsympathetic author. In the long run, not being able to determine good from evil! The writer of literature, of course, becomes helpless, no matter what his intentions might be.

The nonlistener, the nonreader, is a slave to advertising, cheap politicking, and slick pseudoreligious ministration: *to sell something— whether a product, a system, or a donation—the object is to make the target feel empty.* Well-armed, on the other hand, with self-knowledge, insight, confidence, and self-respect (the by-products of the literary experience), we are less susceptible to the tricks of those who find it profitable to exploit us. I could have found the words to soothe those in the auditorium that day; I could have found the code words, neutraliz-ing the students and making them feel good enough to fall back into the soothing daydream of deliteracy. But I was there to read literature, to expose the power of the word, even if, as I would sadly discover, there was no way in that social realm for some to determine friend from foe!

(Ironically, because of the Geneva kids' need to understand and my need to explain, we got together in a classroom and got to know each other. I brought them some of the poetry from a few city high school basketball stars—guys they had played against during the year. Some went on to write their own poems—and I could see that each new phrase of their spontaneous self-expression was more meaningful than any hour of lecturing I could deliver on the power of the written word. Yes, one on one, we developed a real interest in "hearing one out," sharing a bit of our lives with each other—just what I was trying to do when I wrote "America's Pastime.")

And what have poor educators done to try to distinguish between the language that enlightens and the language that deceives? In the name of expediency, they have blurred such a distinction even more. Many col-leges have replaced English and Literature departments with something called *Communication Arts!*

It may not seem like anything to get excited about until you explore the nature of the two studies. An *English* professor attempts to instruct the student to perceive, through writing and reading, the truth of the written word in order to create honest, universal feedback in the name of insight. A *Communication Arts* professor, responsible not only for language awareness but also for marketing and advertising techniques, often instructs the student on how to *deceive* the reader through lan-guage—not for the sake of discovery or awareness, but to evoke a pre-determined response, usually concocted by a business executive who wants the target to feel empty and, thus, in need of a product.

Those are two different worlds. So when a student comes home with an A in Communication Arts, a parent might refrain from rushing out and buying that student a book of Walt Whitman's poetry; the student may be more interested in a videocassette of *Family Feud* reruns. To reiterate, in the world of *deliteracy*, language is successfully misused— the culture rewards those who use language to deceive others and abandons those who attempt to use language to enlighten.

As a result, we are a society cluttered with antiliterature, and language professors, desperate to create their own territory, make the use of language more uninteresting, difficult, and ambiguous than it was ever meant to be.

But we must remember that a cultural tendency affects everyone, and professors too (however esteemed) serve corporate interests, whether they intend to or not. As a matter of fact, if I were a corporate executive or a government official or anyone in authority with a desire to keep thinkers and real communicators at a safe distance from the populace, I'd put them in a university, keep them occupied with departmental politics, and give them enough money and a literary journal to edit in their spare time.

No, I don't think our poets should make their homes in universities, not permanently anyway, though it has come to be that the university is probably the only comfortable, middle-class situation for America's poets. It is a more crucial time than ever, it seems to me, for poets to be close to their communities—not to be celebrated for their unique place in our culture but to be absorbed by a general public, to reveal to others the core of commonality at the center of the artistic experience. *Why poets?*

Poets are the merchants of intuition, intuition transcribed through words into general awareness. We are living in a world where people, especially our youth, have an increasingly difficult time just seeing the world around them, let alone contemplating whatever the meaning of such observations may be. Our poets—the poets of all ages—make us see the world more clearly, and give us the music and the words that make that vision more accessible to others. In a sense, like all artists, they are subversive: awareness breeds change as well as celebration. But they represent an affirmation of life, the possibility of betterment, and a strange optimism in the midst of a society darkened by the clouds of skepticism. The question is, how will the poets survive?

A few years ago I wrote a column for the *Chicago Tribune* trying to make a case for maintaining and actually reviving the arts in our schools. The following day I received a phone call from a woman who said she had grown up and had gone through schools in Japan. She did not need a study to inform her that Japanese students were better educated than our students here. But what she claimed helped me understand more fully our own predicament.

She said the Japanese excel in technology *because of their commitment to education in the arts!* In Japan, a student is exposed early and repeatedly to art and literature—critically, historically, and through personal application. It is an essential part of their schooling. The students not only study the arts, they systematically and continually try their hand at painting, drawing, and poetry. They develop an eye and a mind for *detail,* for *abstract thinking,* for *spatial relationships,* for *technical strategies.* These are not only the elements of lingual and visual arts; they also represent the personal skills that create self-assurance, awareness, and most importantly, *perspective*—just what was missing when I read my story to the students in Geneva that day.

In other words, the Japanese students see, as a matter of conditioning, *the relationship between the world they live in and the world they create!* It seems that Americans, before we complain about educational systems, should acknowledge that today's cultural biases make for tomorrow's cultural environment.

To me—writer, educator, community public servant—the question comes back to the one that opened this chapter: *Who owns the language?* Does it belong to the people? Can they use it, as they would ordinary tools, to repair and decorate the basic shelters of their emotional and intellectual well-being?

Or does language itself, like so many other things, belong to the commercial, corporate world? Is it available to us only in some sterilized, homogenized, prepackaged form, which leaves us content as consumers, but empty as human beings?

Draw a line across the top of a sheet of paper. Attach to that line two arrows, each pointing to the margins. Next to the arrow at the left-hand margin write the word *resources;* next to the arrow on the right-hand margin write the word *destination.* Above the line, write the word *journey.*

I remind the members of the workshop—whether young people or senior citizens—that we are constantly on our way toward something, but always reaching back to something from our past. Each moment, I remind them, is tentative, as we lean forward, or lean back, trying to understand how we got to where we are. I explore for a moment the varying levels of both *destination* (a street corner, the end of the highway, adulthood, a fulfilled human being) and *resources* (money in your pocket, geographical knowledge, knowing how to build a fire, the proper vocabulary to speak of your needs). In other words, I introduce that fine line between the physical and the metaphorical, a "journey" as a convenient vehicle for a natural blend of the two.

I ask each student to imagine the line they have drawn to be a river, or a road, or a path, or anything along which he or she is making a journey. I ask that the first concern be creating the physical presence of that journey—what their feet are touching, what exists on either side of them as they make their way forward, whether it is daylight or twilight or evening, what sounds they hear, etc. I remind them that there is something always tugging at them—their past—and that each step forward is a step into or out of the resources within. I remind them that each discovery along the way should be a discovery for the reader as well. I give them a few words that avail themselves to metaphor and the exercise (*echo, curtain, fire, map, guitar, lost, moonlight, shoulders, current, wind, footprints* . . .) and ask them to include a couple somewhere in their poems.

Paul Harper, close to seventy years old, decides his line is a *tightrope*, and it becomes his metaphor to describe not only the senior citizen writing workshop he is a part of, but the nature of poetry and old age:

EDDIE'S TEA
Paul Harper

Friday morning
we do poetry.
Mellow friends,
ripening in meekness,
fruit sweetening
as days shorten,
wisdom fruit
not yet falling.

Walking a tightrope
across Niagara Falls
without worry,
without fear,
without hurry.
In my hands I hold some cookies
and Eddie's warm,
sweet cup of tea.

Peaceful Friday morning,
slowly, happily floating
across a roaring chaos.
Munching cookies,
sipping honey tea.

We've left behind
the fear of falling.

Young Thomas Bolling, ten years old, followed his "line" to the mountains, and seems to understand quite naturally the connection between the outer world and that which lies within:

Everyday when I go
to the mountains
I dig out rubies.
Then at night
I go home and put rubies
into my heart.

Twelve-year-old Diobe Damco lets his "line" become a typical street in his inner-city neighborhood, "happy to be alive," as he says, despite the violence around him, but already old enough, unfortunately, to develop a pessimistic viewpoint:

I take a walk
down a dark street
and hear the echoes of rap songs.
I see bullets fly by,
disappearing into the darkness.
I am happy to be alive, even
with all the guns and gangs,
the sight of blood making me feel
the pain of others beat up and shot.
And when I see even the light
falling down from the sky
like a curtain,
I know things may never change.

Sixteen-year-old Damon Glasgow does not show up at the Flint Street Recreation Center on a Tuesday night, so I visit his house on the way home from class that night. He is "grounded" for something and has to stay home every night for two weeks. My reaction to hearing this is, as one might imagine, pleasurably positive—after all, all kids do something wrong now and then, but how many are privileged enough to be punished in their own household! I give him the assignment individually, and we take some time to discuss his feelings about his own situation. I meet with him the following week and suggest revisions. His "line" too is the street, but through a series of images and symbols, stepping backwards as well as forward, torn between reality and hope, Damon discovers a faith essential to enriched lives, a faith that echoes the nature of poetry—an affirmation of life whatever the environment:

> I take a step backwards
> and all I see
> is a diffused sky.
> My blood flows like a river
> of fear.
> What must I do?
> Go forward, keeping to myself,
> or stand still and see
> what reality is doing to those
> who have a short life?
>
> Lights flash before my eyes
> like a camera of memories.
> I see snapshot after snapshot,
> guns in teenage hands,
> a trail of cocaine right down
> the avenue of addiction,
> dice on the corner,
> beer on the breath of loners.
>
> I look back up to the sky,
> a horrible, bloody horizon that
> does not end with the killings
> of brothers who died for no reason.
> My mind just takes off,

full of amazement that I'm still here
to talk about anything, let alone sing.

But when I close my eyes
and open them quickly,
things begin to change . . .
On the avenue there's silence,
empty spaces, no one there,
graffiti fading from the walls,
and blacks suddenly holding hands,
singing "Lift every voice and sing . . . "
Where do they come from?

When I take a step forward,
the horizon turns into a beautiful crimson.
Instead of my mind taking off
it's my fingertips that fly away,
like a jet soaring into a battle
of happiness.

I hear voices as I keep walking,
forward now.
It gives me chills down my long,
narrow spine, but my head feels like
a hot furnace blazing in the night.
And I am wondering,
am I dreaming, or can this come true,
the trees blossoming,
the houses filled with families,
streets alive with the music of laughter,
and me on my way home.

Seventy-five-year-old Hilda Gill has chosen as her "line" a river, and
something happens inside me when she reads her poem in her quiet,
broken voice to the workshop members. I am struck once more by the
validity of my own words to the group—that there is a profound connection between the object you choose to describe in your poem and

your own developing identity. (Dare I use Eliot's phrase, "objective correlative," and risk ruining the introspective mood her poem has created?) My reaction to her poem, "The River," reminds me that "teachers" must constantly discover the creations that affirm their pronouncements—otherwise, our lectures will petrify, and we will become the most cynical of professionals. Hilda's poem reminds me that our sorrows are reflected most devastatingly in the polluted waters we've created, leaving the sad burden of our foolish ways and putting the sentiments of our private lives in perspective. Her physical portrait of the river elicits the metaphor of the journey, and when we touch those waters through the sensual images of Hilda's writing, we reach into the currents of our own souls.

RIVER
Hilda Gill

I am old and you, older still.
Nor did I know you in your youth,
as you knew me:
joyful at your side,
running ahead, yet always behind.

Had not loving hands lifted me away
I would have joined you.
Your deceit, treachery, fickleness,
made you strong and fearless.

Drops of sunlight touched you,
then hid in slender branches
of willows
that leaned to sway leafy ribbons
to your rhythm.

It was not easy for me to part
from your flowering aisles and
canopies of green,

so I have come back
to sit by you,

dear friend,
and grieve for your sickness,
worse than mine.

No loving hands have cleansed
the filth and stench
heaped upon you.
No sun lights your darkness,
no flowers flourish in tangled weeds;
the willows have laid themselves
on you in dying protection.

I will be gone
with all my pain and sadness
bearable
as I mourn the torturous wounds
you suffer in silence.

For all these poems I find a public forum—for all the privacy of their endeavor, they were written to be shared. Some will be printed and thumbtacked to the bulletin boards at our recreation and community centers. Some will be read to audiences other than the workshops in which they were produced. A couple will make their way (in the wink of my newspaper editor's eye, a man who knows about the dreaded relationship between poetry and the newspaper business) into my monthly human-interest column as enhancements to my own perspectives. And all will appear in the annual anthology produced by the city government, with a foreword by the mayor. I hope they serve to destroy the image of poets as eccentric, silly, and insignificant. They are, I'm convinced, the most valuable contributions of our community at large.

I've held that view for a long time in fact, a view met with grimaces on the faces of just about everyone—businessmen and women, publishers, public servants, and poets themselves! I. A. Richards, in his book titled, aptly, *Practical Criticism,* claims that the poet, the artist, represents the most *normal* of individuals—that he or she tries to satisfy as many desires as possible without them interfering with one another. Thus, such a person must be a master of organization, especially if the appetite for life is a hardy one. The artist must not only live fully, he or she must maintain control enough to sort out and distinguish experience.

In other words, it is *not* eccentricity that drives an artist, it is a sense of *normality intensified.* In a society too preoccupied with stress, security, and survival, normalcy is not easily identified. It has to do, of course, with maintaining the whole being—which includes our emotional and intellectual appetites, not simply physical needs. Our best poets lead us to an integrated existence—often rubbing against the cultural grain of technology's convenient strategy based on binary simplification. It is our poets, our artists, who remind us just how diverse we are. And when we realize the depth of our being, our dreams become a realistic extension of our desires—not a corporate pipe dream of simply attaining possessions, but a dream of human potential, so our correlation between dreamers and poets (as Freud reminded us) seems meaningful and sensible. Indeed, it is poetry that can create respect for the *whole being.*

But even *respect* is not enough. Americans are practical, "material-minded" by nature. The Greek word for poet is *poiētēs*—meaning a *doer* or *maker,* words that imply there is a legitimate task associated with the beautification of language. Indeed, the implication is that the "poem maker" is not only involved in a meaningful activity (which one might define as formalizing intuitive impulse and providing a distributable result), but also in the creation of a *product.*

The product, it seems we have forgotten in America, is the poem itself. It is not the creation of inflated egos and self-possessed personalities whose titles and credentials overwhelm the notion of their product's availability. It is the poem itself that embodies the sensitivity, insight, and life-affirming qualities that suggest the soul of every one, even if the product of one man or one woman. We know enough in America, the metaphysical heartland of supply and demand, to understand that every product requires someone to possess it. A "maker" is not fulfilled until coupled with a receiver.

And there is a yearning out there! Poets sometimes seem the last to recognize it. Corporate marketers spend their days devising plans to exploit these needs. They create the catchphrases, lyrical jinglism, and sentimentality—all the while belittling, not enriching, the human spirit. Our poets retreat, settling into the ridiculous mind-set that their activity is virtuous though no real product is apparent or viable. It is, indeed, a strange perspective to equate uselessness with pride. But I have witnessed it too often.

Instead, I have seen that once the product is revealed, and once it is known that the product can be created by almost anyone with the urge to do so, the *process is reexamined,* and eventually there's a whole new attitude when the pen first touches the page.

JUSTICE

It doesn't take long to discover that concepts learned in high school have little to do with the world that graduates subsequently encounter.

Don't get me wrong, I knew we were guilty about one thing; I guess I realized that the horse trails in Durand Eastman Park were not meant for motorcycles. But being Catholic and teenagers, we thought anything that was fun was either illegal or immoral, so we made the best of it, Warren trying to maneuver his bulky Honda, and me, on my Triumph, keeping my eyes open for puddles and branches and, of course, horse you-know-what.

Actually, the hilly, winding roads in Durand Eastman Park are as pleasant as the trails themselves, and it didn't take us long to make our way back onto them. Just as we did, slowly banking one of the graceful curves on the road, an oncoming car stopped and some guy got out of it and began waving his arms. We slowed down as we passed him—but seeing the man's angry gestures and hearing his inarticulate shouting, we looked at each other, nodded, and kept going our way. It was best, I remember thinking, not getting involved with a lunatic while on a motorcycle, which, in some instances, could leave you pretty vulnerable.

Some minutes later, riding side by side on Ridge Road heading west, we wondered—going slow enough, I should add, to talk to one another on the cycles—who the guy had been and what he'd wanted.

It didn't take us long to find out. At first we heard a siren. Glancing behind we saw a car quickly closing up on us, speeding and halfway over the white line in the middle of Ridge Road. By the time we realized what was going on, we were being forced not only to the side of the road, but right onto the front lawn of some guy's property.

Warren stalled out. I managed to keep my Triumph running, but I wasn't going anywhere. The maniac in the car jumped out and darted toward us with something held out in his hand. It looked like a badge. It was the same guy who had tried to stop us in the park. I don't remember what he yelled at us, but I guess it was that badge or whatever it was that made us dig out our driving licenses, which he grabbed out of our hands and stuffed in his pocket.

"Follow me," he said. And still dazed we followed him up to Goodman Street where we turned right, down King's Highway, past the intersection of Titus Avenue and left into the parking lot of Irondequoit Town Hall.

Now I often ask myself what made us—streetwise dudes from the club-fisted, muscle-minded territories of Skinny's, Al's Green Tavern, and The Bay and Goodman Grill—what made us so compliant and submissive on that May afternoon in Irondequoit, voluntarily following a complete stranger into a courthouse surely antipathetic to a couple of teenagers on motorcycles. After all, we were only a couple miles from Skinny's. I mean, if this guy had followed us into the parking lot there, the only thing following him out of it would have been his own anxiety regarding the extent of his bruises or the estimate for a car peppered with boot heels and crow bars.

The truth is we learned to be tough—and subsequently confident, self-assured, and surprisingly reasonable and fair-minded—in the familiar surroundings of our own neighborhood. The slightest distance away from it, we became tentative and unresponsive—the rest of the world, in our isolated minds, relied on a power base that excluded us. I'll never forget that ride to Irondequoit Town Hall that afternoon. Warren and I did not look at each other, as we usually did riding side by side on our motorcycles. It was a matter of respect—or perhaps the fear of its loss.

We were charged with speeding and given a court date if we wanted to dispute it. The old guy who commandeered us was an off-duty game warden from the Town of Irondequoit. That was the badge he'd been flashing. I guess riding on the horse trails wasn't enough of a charge for his liking—to which we would have readily admitted. But we were not speeding.

Bobby, Frankie, Joey, and Kenny took their seats in the back rows of the courtroom the night of our trial. Also there to cheer us on was an older gentleman who owned the property on Ridge Road where we had been forced off the road by the vigilante game warden. He had seen us coming down Ridge Road as well that afternoon, and he volunteered to say that we were going slow and certainly not speeding by any means. I had spent the three weeks that had gone by preparing for the case. Essential to our case was Warren's promise not to say anything and screw things up. My strategy, if one could call it that, was to present ourselves as honest and sincere, admit to being on the horse trails and coming across the unmarked car and plainclothes game warden in Durand Eastman Park, and presenting our witness who would testify that we were not speeding and were endangered by the reckless actions of the frantic game warden on Ridge Road.

But when the game warden walked into the courtroom in full, formal, uniform dress—regal and decorated with more patches, stripes, and badges than a born-again Eagle Scout—I knew we had lost.

The judge listened—even allowed me to use a portable blackboard to draw a map of our route from the park to Ridge Road. He let us explain that the arresting citizen was not identified as a game warden, nor was his car designated in any way. The game warden, meanwhile, his brass and silver buttons and badges reflecting the light like a third-world artifact, sat there calmly and barely attentive. We brought our witness up and he testified—under oath, of course—to what he saw. Warren became a little anxious and spontaneously offered a comment—only to be told by the judge that the word was "irrelevant," not "irreverent," as Warren had blurted out.

I thought our case had gone well, and I sat in my chair in front of the judge waiting for the prosecution to make its case. But before I could look back for some thumbs-up encouragement from my friends, the game warden made his remark and was already heading back to his chair. "They were speeding your Honor—I did all I could do to catch up to them," he said. And before I could cough up an allusion to his contradiction of our third-party witness to the whole affair, I heard the judge pronounce succinctly and with conviction his judgment:

"Defendants guilty. Fine, thirty dollars each and your licenses marked with the conviction."

It was at that moment I uttered what now strikes me as the only legitimate response an individual is capable of in the midst of what is conceived as a higher power, be it state or church: to the judge I said, astonished, "How can you say that?"

It was a few months later when I discovered a couple of postscripts to the affair. On the day of the "citizen's arrest," I went to our family lawyer for advice—after all, I remember telling Warren, "there must be something in the legal system we can appeal to, I mean justice is justice." But the lawyer said, regretfully, shaking his head sadly and lighting up one of his expensive cigars with a gold initialed lighter, that there was nothing he could do. Then he wished us luck when I told him I'd go to court myself and explain it all to the judge.

But about three months later he told my mother, who went to him about another matter, that he could have gotten us off with a phone call—that, indeed, since it was a citizen's arrest involving a private automobile, all we needed to ask for at the trial was a verification of the accuracy of the man's speedometer within forty-eight hours of the arrest. "But Gina," he said, in his friendly, expensive manner, "kids on motorcycles need to be taught a lesson."

And there was another lesson too—which I learned about a couple of months after our "conviction." I was telling the story of the bogus speed rap to my cousin Chuck who was the produce manager of the A & P at the Goodman Shopping Center. When I mentioned game warden and described the guy, Chuck laughed and shook his head. It turns out the man was caught shoplifting not once but twice in Chuck's store. Apparently he didn't attempt to get his side of it heard in the court at Irondequoit Town Hall where he could show up with a chest full of metal; he paid off the store to keep the matter quiet instead. His word, echoing regally through the Halls of Justice, against ours!

To tell the truth, my view hasn't mellowed much over the years. Justice, it seems, is still more a convenience of the powerful than a cornerstone of the people. I just wish I'd been given a few more years rather than a mere impressionable eighteen to think of the nation as indivisible with justice and liberty for all. Because it wasn't so much the humiliation, or even the conviction, which was a mere slap on the wrist for all those original sins we were born with. And it wasn't even the extra hundred dollars I had to pay for each of three years for car insurance due to the mark on my license. No, it was something more than that as we stood under oath, jittery but with hope, our loss for words less and less a handicap as we gained the courage to simply speak out in the name of truth. Perhaps, Warren, "irreverent" was the right word after all, because our spirit was broken a bit that night.

And it is too bad that the only light left in my memory from our courtroom initiation is the glittering, starry reflections from the game warden's badges and commendations.

One morning in Chicago, just as I was jotting down a few notes in a poetry anthology for the class I would be teaching at Loyola University that afternoon, the phone rang.

It was Rod McKuen.

Now this sentence I have just written—*It was Rod McKuen*—this beginning to a serious chapter on the role of poetry in America, would certainly bring a smile to many of my poet-acquaintances throughout the country—because, of course, in the academic mind of poetry, it is difficult to take such a sentimentalist rhyme-maker seriously, even if the guy has sold more contemporary poetry books than any other poet in the history of America.

As a matter of fact, I brought sneers to the faces of poets and critics when, during a couple of panel discussions over the past few years, I've made the observation that if poetry survives at all in America, perhaps more credit will go to Rod McKuen than to any of a few high-powered poetry critics.

Do I say these things because I am a fan of Rod McKuen's? No, not really. I'd be the first to say his poetry is filled with overused, often trite phrases, sentimentalism, predictability, and a naive, terribly romantic view of the world. But I do admire other aspects of the man.

McKuen is a man who believed in himself as a poet. More than that, he believed that poets could find a place in the hearts of Americans, and he committed himself—by putting, literally, everything he had on the line in order to make his poetry accessible to many instead of a few. He knew something about the needs of people, and when he made his way up the California coast, talking bookstore owners into carrying and displaying his books, he began to touch a vital chord in a land where poetry had made itself so incredibly inaccessible and hard to find. And people from all backgrounds began responding to his books, buying them in astounding numbers—in a manner not dissimilar from the way European and South American poets, like Neruda (and his small first collection *Twenty Love Poems and A Song of Despair*), caught on among the populace; or the way in which poetry collections are purchased by the thousands by common people throughout Eastern Europe and the former Soviet Union.

The argument is, of course, that McKuen sold well because he was such a bad poet, giving the public birthday verse instead of an intellectual experience. I, for one, wish that McKuen were a better poet—*but I don't think his sales would have fallen off if he were a better poet!* If he were terribly vague, or unduly private, that's another matter. But McKuen did his best, like a *good* romance novelist, and furthermore he sensed an incredible void in the material made available to the reading public in this country. The fact is, unless materials exist—in this case a body of work that is available for some collective evaluation that goes beyond the Southern poetry critic's "fifty patrons"—it will be impossible to observe the decorums of rank and precedence of poetry in America. For our country's poets who seem to flourish without an identifiable or meaningful audience (namely, our university poets who make a claim to their titles and status anyway) the lack of a readership becomes, in my mind, a justification for any kind of writing that may seem mediocre or inaccessible or just plain uninteresting—in other words, insulating themselves against any criticism by taking the position that if a poem isn't effective, it is ultimately the fault of an ignorant readership. Criticism then becomes, as Thomas M. Disch observes in an article for *The Nation*, "an exchange of favors and courtesies, written in the bloated language of blurbs."

So I was pleased to be talking with Rod McKuen that morning. I had invited him to meet with my poetry workshop, and though ultimately we could not arrange a convenient time to do so, we spoke for quite a while, and I was surprised to see how anxious he was to be accepted by the so-called "literary circle of poets" who spent a lot of their time trashing him. I sensed that dark, sad, huge gap in this country between writers who possessed valid literary credentials but lacked a readership, and those, like McKuen, who lacked those credentials but had an audience that could confirm those credentials (if indeed they existed) through some meaningful response to their writings.

I asked myself again: why, in a country so hungry for the brief intensity of the emotional and insightful moment, hungry for voices at once familiar yet refreshing that convey a spark of awareness . . . why are the poets in America so invisible?

Ironically, I ended up in Washington, D.C., hoping to put some of the puzzle together.

In the spring of 1989, the Folger Library sponsored a symposium entitled "On History's Doorstep: The Role of Poetry in Society." It was also a tribute to our then poet laureate, Howard Nemerov, both the poet himself and the title he held. There was a good, broad array of panelist writers, including, among others, Lucille Clifton, a powerful and popular black poet; Andre Codrescu, the eccentric and poetic voice heard on PBS's *All Things Considered;* Carolyn Forche, a poet whose Nicaragua-based book of poetry sold more copies than Harper & Row ever imagined; and my old friend guru, populist, and government administrator all in one—Gary Snyder.

Of course the first thing I noticed sitting in the audience during the opening session, "The Changing Role of Poetry," was that all the wrong people were sitting there with me! It was, predictably, an audience filled with poets, most of whom I sensed were longing for some sort of recognition that might approach that of the poets on the panel; people not nearly so interested in the "role of poetry" as they were in their own personal roles. The woman next to me, the first person I talked to at the conference, handed me some brochure about a reading series she ran in Virginia, asked me if I were a writer, and within five minutes issued me an invitation to give a reading there if I were in the vicinity sometime. She told me too where her poems were published, and it became obvious that this event was probably seen as a chance for "networking" among those who felt disenfranchised in the silent world of poetry.

Perhaps that's what these literary events were meant to be, but since I was experiencing poetry as a vehicle for social awareness in Rochester—and not in an elitist club atmosphere but in the realm of public forum—I was hoping that the discussion would develop toward the social instead of the personal specter.

In a way, it began to. Eliot Weinberger, moderator of the first session, seemed to get right to the heart of the problem of ineffectiveness on the part of our "poetry community." He described the middle-class comforts of our university poets, with plenty of jobs and small magazines to manufacture credentials; he described this willing isolation of writers from communities, saying "America has created a sealed cage with plenty of cheese." I couldn't agree more, but Weinberger's views were not popular with an audience bent on celebrating its own existence. As a matter of fact, the only other view during the conference that met with equal unpopularity was Lewis MacAdam's idea that a poet laureate had responsibilities that could be applied directly to the social awareness of poetry. Perhaps, it struck me, as I witnessed such disinterest in ideas that seemed to be at the heart of this conference's probe, the title should have been changed from "The Role of Poetry in Society" to "The Celebration of Poets in a Limited Setting."

Others, though, did try to put things into some perspective. Lucille Clifton, for example, felt compelled to bring up the question of *how to be poets,* or *what poets do,* rather than the overly indulged question of how to write poetry. Her definition of poets seemed apt: people who commit themselves passionately to something. And it seemed right too that we would have to be reminded of that here at the center of a middle-class, technology-bent society, where the notion lingers that technical training, not emotional investment, is the key to revealing as well as exhibiting ability. It seemed right too that these poets should hear this from a black woman in her fifties. Lucille Clifton's poetry comes deep from experience, alive not from the cool, objective eye of

confessionalism, but from the passion of total exposure; not just report-
age, but a devotion to revealing both a sensibility to a life of suffering
and love, and to a graceful, beautiful rendering of a voice at once
distinctive and universal. However lyrical her image, however vulnerable her subject matter, Clifton is honest and straightforward—which
is, after all, the final requirement for those who commit themselves
passionately to something or someone. If I had to pick out one group
that represented the goodness of the American character, it would be
black females born between 1900 and 1945. This is a group that knows
hardship and responsibility, a group that epitomized the collective roles
of workers, parents, and household keepers in this country. And this
group accepted its role in a most generous, caring, hostility-free manner, making few demands but maintaining family and home against, at
times, incredible disruptive forces. If poetry rises here—that strained
utterance, that affirmation of life—then there is hope for everyone.

It is ironic, then, to report the thrust of this particular panel's assessment of the role of the poet in America. Andre Codrescu and Gary
Snyder began describing our culture in terms of a *center*, with the core
more intense and the periphery sparse in comparison. The center was
bloated with hostility, greed, material concerns, etc.—a place where
sensitive, more giving souls such as poets could not be found. All the
poets on the panel, indeed, agreed that poets could be found on the
margin of the circle, on the periphery of the culture's center, making
sure the outside is alive, distinct from what they described as the busy
but vacuous core. There was, ironically, a certain glee in their voices, a
certain pride in their acknowledgment that they were on the outside of
the circle looking in, celebrating the fact *as if they actually had chosen to
be there!*

Let me state why these poets might celebrate being on the margin of
the culture's circle: I expect such satisfaction comes from poets who
have soft, cozy positions at universities where you can have little or no
effect on the community and still call oneself a "writer-in-residence,"
and earn a paycheck and gather the respect of those who are never
affected by a single poem (if they ever read poetry at all, that is). These, I
imagine, are the poets who might celebrate being on the periphery of

cultural activity because not only can they make a living, more importantly, they never have to test the waters of the community to see if they
are making any kind of a difference with their writing, a difference in
the way others might gain insight from a literary experience. Indeed,
without a readership, there is no literary experience. So these poets can
write when they want to, if they want to, and they can find lots of
publication opportunities that provide them not with an identifiable
readership or a chance for feedback, but with enough credentials to
maintain their status and positions. This routine, of course, mirrors
many academia efforts—the unread dissertations, the barrage of mean-
ingless paper-reading sessions, etc.—and the picture should be clear: by
engaging in this "poetry for poetry's sake" situation, one is not on the
margin of the culture's center, one is in the very thick of its core: the
cynical acceptance of art as a respectable but useless vehicle in our
society's bleak and nasty agenda of priorities. Weinberger's ignored
remark—"a sealed cage with plenty of cheese"—kept reverberating in
my mind.

The entire conference—"The Role of Poetry in Our Society"—origi-
nated, I imagine, because there is a real, a crucial question in the minds
of many about whether there is any role at all. I sensed in the audience
made up of people who wanted desperately some acknowledgment of
their own commitments to poetry that although they applauded their
poet counterparts on the panel (needing, of course, a celebrated model
with whom to identify), underneath there was a genuine seething, an
anger, a feeling of uselessness, transparency, abandonment by the culture—an anger that would eventually be misdirected and find its way
into the bloated hostile center that the poets on the panel could keep, at
least in their minds, from falling into. No, the audience didn't buy, I
sensed, the idea of celebrating the straddling of the margin. It seems to
me that the role of poets, of all artists, is to commit themselves, as
Lucille Clifton suggested, to a passionate attempt to try and make their
way to the center of the culture—forays if not inhabitance—and subvert
the disturbing powers within, disrupting at times the cynical business of
the system and celebrating not the distance one can keep from the
intensity of life, but that life itself, whenever it can be affirmed.

The discussions, I'm sad to say, became even more ludicrous during the conference. The occasion also marked a tribute to our poet laureate, Howard Nemerov, who was included on one of the final panel sessions—the one that Lewis MacAdams tried unsuccessfully to start off on a serious note regarding responsibility. The discussion turned quickly into a big joke, with Gary Snyder reciting a list of goodies that should be made available to the poet laureate—such as a yacht, an unlimited American Express card, a suite at the finest Hawaiian hotel, etc. It was all in good fun, and the audience of would-be poets laughed and applauded at the fantasies. As a matter of fact, the fantasy list seemed the appropriate conclusion to the conference, since it served to amplify the many mini-fantasies of recognition among the audience. Again, the emphasis was the celebration of poets, not the meaningful distribution of the poetic sensibility throughout the community.

Howard Nemerov, ironically, seemed perfectly comfortable with the jest, and it reminded me of my first contact with him when I was a student at Syracuse University and he looked over some student poetry at a workshop—where he took a quick look at a couple of things and, grumbling something under his breath, said finally that all he could say was that "all undergraduate poetry was as cute as a bug's ear." I don't know the extent of the cynicism behind that remark, but it seemed that all this fuss over poets and so little concern about the role poetry might or might not play in our society was similarly "as cute" and as inessential as the poetry such disregard might inspire.

In December of 1989, a twenty-three-year-old black man named Chris Tuck was shot and killed in front of his home around midnight. It did not surprise a lot of people in Rochester, New York—not neighbors, acquaintances, or policemen who knew Chris. He had been constantly in trouble since a shoplifting incident during his final year in high school, graduating to more serious criminal activities, and finding his way frequently to tough crowds, courtrooms, and even jail. In a way, it was a typical direction for a tough, inner-city kid, but Chris was someone special, so for days after his death he was the center of newspaper and television features.

Chris Tuck had been the most talented basketball player ever to come out of the Rochester area. He was, in high school, by all accounts, "a man among boys," and led his team to two high school state championships. The shoplifting incident, though, led to his suspension in his senior year, and that marked the beginning of the demise of his basketball career. He tried making it at a community college and a couple of state colleges, but he kept being drawn back to his old neighborhood and the criminal life he couldn't seem to shake. Finally, his toughness was no match for the ease of a trigger finger, and when he died, it was evident to an entire city that even tremendous ability such as Tuck's could not insure a break from a bleak, tragic life.

I first met Chris Tuck in the spring of 1985. The poetry/basketball program was just beginning in Rochester recreation centers. It was my idea to bribe the inner-city youth by allowing them the use of the gym *only* if they took part in a poetry-writing workshop beforehand. This was met, as one might imagine, with some bewilderment by the kids at the centers—as well as by equally bewildered, often cynical recreation staff members when asked to cooperate with the program.

Who is this guy anyway? read the faces of the kids at the first centers I visited. It seemed, absolutely, the right question to ask—not just of me, a poet with a basketball in one hand and a notebook in another, but of all poets, who must, in the end, relate the fiction of their lyrical assessments with the fact of common experience. It was a question I welcomed, because in my own beginnings I was told that poetry was for "special beings," and yet although I could write (and publish!) as well as the next poet in America, I didn't feel "special," but adversely tuned in to a universal spirit that had more to do with a sensibility nurtured from the humble environment of my past.

Part of my insistence in my first contract with the city was that I be given paid time to ingratiate myself into certain environments, because at the heart of poetry is *trust* and its counterpart *honesty.* After all, I said to myself, not sure just how philosophical a city commissioner might be, it was the challenge of the times for poets—if they were to be respected and appreciated in any legitimate manner in America, *they had to make themselves accessible to the public at large.*

So I hung around, played some ball, and began getting to know some of the kids at the youth centers where I had planned to start a program. Of course I got to know the staff at these centers as well—because they had had as much contact with writers and poetry as the kids—*none!* I felt all the ghosts of the years of stereotyping poets hanging on my arms and legs. The staff wanted to know, it struck me, if I was an "alright guy"; the kids wanted to know if I could "ball." I couldn't help thinking that somehow poets in this country had managed to hide away so effectively they had become in the minds of others ethereal caricatures of enormous dimension.

One afternoon as the workshops were to begin, I agreed that anyone who could beat me one-on-one in basketball didn't have to attend the workshops in order to play ball later. Fortunately, I had a good day—the jumper was falling, and everybody except one lanky fellow attended the workshop (and five minutes later he came in too—to "see what was going on"). Another time, feeling a little tired, I made a game of Ping-Pong the test of workshop attendance.

Chris Tuck, though, needed no such prompting. I told him straight out that his participation—because he was so respected for his basketball talent—would encourage others to try out their imaginations and create voices as distinct as jump shots. He joined the younger kids in a room off the gym in one of our city's recreation centers. I began by introducing a couple of short, effective poems—one by Etheridge Knight, the other by Lucille Clifton—that the kids had never heard before. As a matter of fact, they were surprised to hear poems to which they could relate and respond—contemporary poems involving subject matter and language relevant to their own experience. I then made my pitch for their own creative efforts, their own distinct voices, and provided a ten-minute word game that enabled them to stumble onto image and metaphor, even if merely by chance.

Oddly enough, for the first time ever, Chris Tuck's mother came to the recreation center to find her son that afternoon. She was astonished to hear that he was in a back room "writing poetry" with some other boys! Suspicious, she stomped back to the room and was even further astonished to see her strapping six-foot-five star athlete of a son hunched over a piece of paper and scratching at it with a pencil. Here's the poem Chris wrote that day:

FAST BREAK

When I let go
of the ball I hear
the swish of the river
as it flows behind my back.
The stars and the moon stick
like knives in a mirror.
On a fast break I stumble
into the tall grass,
and I hear my voice
getting shaky.

When I read Chris's poem the first time, I was taken immediately by the last lines: "I hear my voice getting shaky." It was, of course, a shaky time for Chris—freshly suspended from the team after the shoplifting episode, no team to play for, his future ballplaying days in doubt.

Chris was often criticized for his toughness, his arrogance. I saw a more gentle side. He seemed at times almost apologetic for the immense physical strength that was his trademark. Reflective moments—like writing a poem—bring out qualities that otherwise might go unacknowledged in someone (that is, in fact, one of the main purposes of the community creative writing program I began). When I look again at Chris's poem, I see that even at the moment of glory ("letting go of the ball") he imagines the "swish" as the sound of another environment—"the river flowing" and "stumbling into the tall grass"—which is, curiously, what many people said Chris needed all along.

He did try playing ball at a college in Kansas, but that lasted only a few weeks. The closer-to-home state college (SUNY at Brockport) seemed okay for Chris for a short time, but he couldn't handle the academic work, and his old neighborhood kept drawing him back. I even talked to my friend Gene Sullivan, basketball coach at Loyola University in Chicago, where I was a professor for several years; but that too was futile.

In his poem, even the stars and moon, objects that reflect someone's dreams and hopes, stick menacingly "like knives" in the self-reflecting images of the mirror. When *dreams* hurt a person, how far away is a tragic burst of that dream, or the shattering of an image? It is no wonder Chris ended his "Fast Break" with a shaky voice. I get a little nervous too—seeing the life of a youth slip away like that, a young man who possessed so much God-given physical talent, the envy of so many.

And I think of how so many of our youth will encounter the troubles of a Chris Tuck, and how many will die tragic young deaths, and how their lives will not make the news, and how few people will ever know how these young people existed . . .

During the same year Chris died it turned out that three of the top basketball players in the city had been members of the creative writing workshops in our city recreation program. All of them had had poems published in our annual collections, and some of their poems had appeared in newspaper features as well. Of course the general public knew these kids as ballplayers.

I thought it might be a good idea for others to see these kids' creative efforts printed on the page as well—especially since Martin Luther King, Jr. Day was coming up and I wanted to get across to the kids in the schools that King was, among other things, an elegant poet whose voice was filled with the gutteral lyricism of the black experience: a singer of hardship, a carrier of the excruciating melody of hope against a background of despair. So, as part of our recreation program, we published a booklet of poetry from our poetry/basketball program. In it were the poems of, among others, Herman Humphries, Lashon Nathon, and LeRoy Brown, the three top scorers in the city high school basketball league—kids who were among the first to write poems in our recreation program.

We visited two middle schools (grades six to eight) and passed out booklets of poems, gave readings, and even made trips to the gyms of the schools where these young poet-ballplayers gave tips and an exhibition in shooting to the younger kids. Suddenly the images of jump shots and dunks were being complemented by the reflective images of words. young Markel Peaks reading his poem,

I'm still trying to reach America,
but as I walk, it seems I'm
getting further away.
The world seems like I'm not
in it anymore, because I don't see
anyone . . . just beautiful Markel, walking,
trying to clutch onto the world.

And Renell Cleveland, reading his words about not being able to
"hide behind a fence that surrounds my feelings"; he continues:

. . . in the morning, broke, all I see
is other people with the same problem,
a man, old, wrinkled, through—
not really a man;
and a boy, looking around,
wondering in a world too large,
everything so new and difficult . . .

I too wonder,
is this the beginning
of a boy becoming a man?

Herman Humphries, an intimidating six-foot-six leaper, reads
softly a sensitive juxtaposition of adventure and the stable love of a
mother:

. . . I'm 3 years old, coming home
to my mother, trying to memorize
which apartment door to go to . . .

And from the same poem:

. . . I see nothing in sight but a
small light at the end of the road,
a headlight, someone to drive off with.
I start walking towards it because
I think this is the way out of this
little world I'm in . . .

And the clever but insightful couplet at the end of six-foot-five Lashon Nathan's poem:

> Life isn't a swim through wealth;
> it's a muddy struggle through poverty.

I could see in the eyes of the middle school students a transition taking place. There was a connection being made that allowed them to see not only these ballplayers differently, but themselves. There was an elegance in the words, an inner grace that gave the whole being its due respect. It was, in my mind, a kind of magic—not just the magic of an individual pulling out of the empty air a beautiful identity. But the magic of literature—of poetry; the enlightenment through words of the human condition, the suffering, the joy. In Goethe's words, "If I have to live a life of anguish and agony, I thank God for a voice to speak of it."

These young people, writers and listeners, became the literary experience that somehow eludes our educators. It came from a combination strange to most: personal investment, imaginative experimentation, and a trust in poetry and the voices it creates.

Karee McGill, a sixteen-year-old ballplayer reads his poem, and when I hear it, I realize that he has said in a poem called "Ball," in a few words of poetry, what is essential for those listening to understand.

BALL

> As I dribble and pull up
> for a shot
> the image faded
> and I remember I am in
> my bathroom shooting a towel
> in the dirty clothes hamper.
> I think, instead,
> I can fix the toilet,
> and I can feed my children.
> Ball was a dream.

All the poems in this chapter appeared in *Rochester Voices: Uncommon Writings from Common People,* Rochester's fifth-year anniversary collection of writings from youth and senior citizens. It also contained oral history transcriptions and stories from such people as the city's police chief and a popular black city councilwoman. In March of 1990, several months after the book was published and distributed throughout the community, I was informed that the school district had purchased six hundred copies for classroom use. That meant, of course, that the creative expressions of members of the community would be the subject matter in our area's classrooms—so there would be a very good chance that a neighbor's poetry, or a classmate's, or a friend's or family member's, or even a grandparent's, or just a person someone knew, would be studied as legitimate literature—*indeed, just what it was meant to be.*

Make a list of weather-related words—*fog, rain, icicle, thunder, wind,* etc.—say fifteen or twenty of them. In an adjacent column, make a list of body-related words—*fingertips, brow, heart, shoulders, voice,* etc. In a third adjacent column, make a list of abstract words that represent ideas so vast in concept they constantly change in meaning, requiring re-definitions as identities change—*love, regret, wisdom, ignorance, loneliness, disillusion, joy,* etc.

Pick one of the weather words and write it down on a blank page (e.g., *icicle*). After it, write a verb that commonly goes with the weather word (icicle *melting*). Now scan the second column, the body words, and describe where the first phrase is taking place using one of the listed words (icicle melting *in the heart*). Finally, write the preposition *of* after the body word noun (icicle melting in the heart *of*) and examine the last column of words, the abstractions. Ask yourself what abstraction might describe the concept of the image you've created, and write it after the word *of*—an icicle melting in the heart, for example, suggests a feeling of melancholy, or perhaps icicle melting in the heart of loneliness, which is, thus, the "magical" phrase that arises out of the word game.

Of course there are numerous possibilities, and the ease of invention is as essential in this exercise as the resulting poetic phrase. This is, in fact, an exercise that illustrates both the playfulness of imagination and the verbal wordplay inherent in *imagery*. It illustrates the connection between chance and discovery, the essential poles of a writer's latitude. Eventually, I encourage the students to do away with the prepositional phrase, the abstraction itself thus illustrating the power of the image to illicit on its own the prevailing thought or emotion of the poetic rendering. The students experiment—*dust gathering on the shoulders (of ignorance), wind blowing through the eyes (of freedom)* . . . The subconscious rises to the surface, context realizes itself through a lyrical beckoning of imagery, the pen moves effortlessly across the page. "Write first, think later," I say, knowing the muse will forgive such a simplistic statement.

Of course the real secret to motivating people to write is to create the urge to communicate. Artistic expression comes from those who are sincerely reflective, extending their personal worlds beyond the self. The simple act of the literary effort is an acknowledgment of time—the past as resource, the future a test of the validity of perspective. In a society where the exuberance of the moment overwhelms the consideration of a moment's effect on the future, it is difficult to make a case for the importance of literature. But a phone call from the city school district brings me to a classroom where the environment is more than conducive to reflection, consideration, imagination, the elements essential to self-expression.

It is a program called The Young Mothers Program, a program teenagers can attend through their pregnancies without too much of an interruption of their schoolwork. I have been asked to conduct a poetry workshop with the teenage girls there, and during the first workshop I realize that I do not have to fight them to consider the significance of *contemplation.* They already know about extending their world beyond the self—their bodies speak to them; they know the term *sensual awareness* before I use it in class. They have a lot to ponder because they know their lives will not be easy. I recall Mallarmé's phrase, "poetry is the language of a state of crisis." And yet there is a sense of joy within them; it is, of course, the anticipation of giving birth, a celebration of life itself. One of those quirky, undeniable phrases comes to my mind, the kind one never utters in public—"motherhood is poetry," I say to myself, as I glance at the concentrated expressions on the faces of these young girls.

HISTORY
Niteria Holley

Everything seems ready to
give birth
as I read this book that is
open in my lap.
The words give birth
to history . . . and as I read
I find that history
has not passed.
It will last and be remembered,
like the clock I look upon
reminds me
of my past.
I realize I too
am a book,
with words that tell
a story.

THE BLACK BALLOON
Erica Wilson

Like a dark tunnel, imagine
being in a black balloon, unable
to come out until you mature.

You start to think
it is a life of no worries
in that balloon, your mother's uterus.

I, on the other hand,
have lots to worry about,
making you the best child I can,
feeding you healthy, nurturing
strong bones and skin beautiful.

So my child I tell you this,
you'll always be grateful to me

and your father, because you
were a part of us, and still are.

So when you see the black balloon,
feel peaceful. It was your first name.

As I read over the poems that will fill the pages of a school district pamphlet entitled "The Body Inside Mine" (poetry that will be re-printed as the center of a Gannett newspaper article and that will enable two hundred thousand conservative readers to consider another view of the dilemma of teenage pregnancies), I realize that these are poems that remind us of our humanity, of the incredible potential for love in the midst of hard times. These girls, whose lives indeed may not be easy, have a few articulate moments with which to remember their pregnan-cies—and their babies will utter their first life-affirming sounds, those cries that emanate from the poetic soul of a species intent on survival. It seems so basic, the urge of these teenage writers: to love and protect their young.

Another phone call to City Hall. To the writer-in-residence at City Hall. A strange place, it seems, as I lift the receiver. An administrator from the state education department calls, asking if I'll give the keynote address to a group of "At-Risk Student" teachers and administrators; a woman calls to ask if I'll look at a diary found in the house of a ninety-five-year-old neighbor who's just been placed in a nursing home. A local Grange member asks if I'll address a meeting in a small town thirty miles southwest of the city; Nazareth College calls to schedule a seminar for area teachers; a young woman calls to get the dates for the next work-shop for writing poetry; a social worker calls to see if I'll look over the writing of a troubled teenager who's living in a halfway house; someone wants to donate books to a recreation center. The city historian calls to confirm our agenda for a course in rediscovering Rochester's monu-ments that is cotaught with me and offered free to teenagers and senior citizens. A television station calls to set up studio time to complete another youth poetry-video that will appear as a news program feature; an old gentleman calls and asks if we could send him a copy of this year's anthology of writings by area residents. The *Today Show* calls to say that Katie Couric and her crew will arrive on a Tuesday morning; the daughter of one of our senior citizen writers calls and asks if I would deliver the eulogy and read one of her mother's poems at the funeral mass on Friday morning.

This time it is a director from the Rochester Museum and Science Center. To complement an exhibit that will feature an area migrant woman, an exhibit that uses the poetry of our elderly black women from the oral histories program, would I like to arrange for some of my young writers to put together an exhibit of poetry, photographs, and artifacts that illuminate the lives of inner-city children?

It will become the *first time* the city and the museum work in conjunction on a project. Eastman Kodak, upon my request, provides cameras, film, developing, and enlargements for the exhibit which, completed less than six months after the initial phone call, is called "Urban Expressions," a spectacular graffiti wall upon which appear original poems of youth, their photographs of their environment, photographic portraits of them, and many of the artifacts that were the subject matter of their poetry—basketball sneakers, a teddy bear, a boom box, a cocaine pipe, a toy sports car, a family photo album, a bedroom mirror, a high school diploma, etc. The exhibit remains for almost a year to the delight of thousands of museum visitors. Something comes clear—that poetry is not just words on a page, it is an emergence of perspective when the connection is made between individuals, environment, and a community (the viewers). On the day the exhibit opens, I watch the sixteen young participants scribble their names in brightly colored markers under their poems and photographs on the graffiti wall. They are, it strikes me, making a claim to the legitimacy of their individual voices— but this time, under the lights of the local television cameras—it is an honor, not a misdemeanor. "I find myself lost among things," reads young Autumn Brady's poem on the wall, right under the old blue blanket she wrote of, which is encased in glass. "I'm trying to wake up," she has written, "but the thing is we're all asleep . . . the whole world is asleep until we wake up to a new side for everyone to see: being unique and not being made fun of anymore." Standing in front of the exhibit wall, I understand what it takes for us to listen to others: a quiet, honorable space with a little well-focused light and a sense of history.

SMOKING THE PIPE
Damon Glasgow

Here I am, lost on the avenue,
staring at all the geekers
on the corner pheming for a hit
of the soft white cocaine.
In spring time when all bums
use the pipe, a voice echoes
through the air saying'
Yo Man, You Got That Girl . . .

When I turn around, I fear
when I get older
I will find myself in jail,
looking down at the
waste in the corner
of a cell.
As I go to the corner in
the afternoon, I picture myself
as cousin Hank, always in jail.

TEDDY BEAR
Terry Gibbs

I look at my teddy bear sitting on
the log in my room. He's brown,
a Koala bear I take to school for
good luck. I got it
when I was born, from my mom.
Every time I look at it
it makes me smile.

I know I'm older now,
and I've outgrown my teddy bear.

But he seems to know me, saying
I love you Terry, stay with me
I need somebody to talk to me.

So he sits on the log,
while I sleep, and grow so fast
into a man.

I read thirteen-year-old Terry's poem over to myself once more on a winter's night almost a year after the exhibit. Across from me, sitting in a corner of my dining room, is his teddy bear, the one that appeared with his poem along the "Urban Expressions" wall. He left town before the exhibit ended and did not leave any new address or notice of his destination. When the exhibit closed, I was given the bear, and I expect I will keep it always—remembering Terry for the sweet kid he was, thinking of how courageous it was to write that kind of poem in the midst of the tough environment of that neighborhood workshop. But he was not teased about it—on the contrary, other kids understood the sentiment, each one of them trying to hold onto something innocent and joyful in the midst of that incredibly rushed journey into the frightening world of manhood.

The next morning I bring the bear and the story of Terry's absence to a group of senior citizens in one of our oral history programs. It inspires one woman, in her seventies, to tell her childhood story (which I transcribed and wrote)—and it reminds us that hard times for the young is of course not simply a recent development. Helen Johnson's story recounts the unspoken moments of a generation, the hidden abuses and fearful silences of a broken family. Her metaphor, the exterior of a beautiful house, represents the grand illusion, the prospering family, we have fostered so long in America.

THE MANSION
story by Helen Johnson
(transcribed and written by Ross Talarico)

My father was a carpenter
and I can see him standing

in the streaks of light
touching the gumwood trim
in the newly-finished sun-parlor.
I can see my mother
holding her hands over the small fire
burning like a stray thought
in the massive brick fireplace.
I see myself
leaning against the leaded glass
of the doors that lead
to the library, the shelves empty of course,
and my vision
a rainbow of confusion . . .

There was no furniture
except some old crates and mattresses.
I made up stories
to keep my friends out
as they walked home from school
and stopped to admire
the stately mansion they called my home.
But it was temporary.
Soon the house was sold, and we moved on,
my father packing his tools.
For a few months we lived well,
enough coal to heat the half-built rooms,
chicken, dried carrots, cabbage
and perogi.
But before long, as the house took shape,
and the walls were plastered,
and the fireplaces bricked, and
the doors fitted with bronze hardware,
it was back to noodles and rice.

And that would have been all right
except for the beatings

and the cold stare of my father
who seemed to love his work
but not his life.
I remember locking a bathroom door
with my mother inside
and hiding the key, and my father
pounding on the door
as he had often pounded on her.
But he would not destroy
such a rich finished oak door.

One day he dragged a steamer trunk
into the barren vestibule
and onto the front porch.
Badz zdrowa, he said, without any emotion
at all; it means, in Polish, *stay well.*
And when a small pick-up truck
pulled up, and he got in,
that's the last we saw of him.
We looked at each other,
at the sparseness of the huge room,
of our lives to that point,
and we held onto each other
until the fire went out.

*S*undays.

I think perhaps it was the peaceful offering of the mystical Latin mass that took it out of us. Or maybe the slow choke-hold of our clumsy dark ties, or even the slower genuflection as we mumbled our way into the temporary humility of the Lord's graces.

Whatever it was, it had to do with our minds or our hearts, because we filled our stomachs with spaghetti and meatballs and Ran Cora's fresh Italian bread . . . and that didn't help any.

There was always a great emptiness that seemed to fill the world on Sunday afternoons. You could see it on the streets, at the gas station where the pumps stood like tombstones on the abandoned corner of Bay and Goodman. You could see it in the eyes of my atheist father who dozed at noon, and in the empty parking lot in front of the A & P at the shopping center; and you could see it everywhere in the hazy sky you inevitably found yourself staring into.

It is no wonder we would shed our good clothes, excuse ourselves from the well-meaning monotony of relatives, and head out in one of our dad's cars for . . . well, for nowhere.

What I mean is we didn't have to come up with a destination or a purpose for our late Sunday afternoon drives. We wouldn't even discuss it. We'd just head down Bay Street to Goodman, take Goodman to Main Street where, after crossing the old Railroad Street Bridge and passing the Dental Dispensary near Alexander Street, we'd slow down, slouch, and comb our hair.

It was the Sunday afternoon Cruise. On this particular Sunday I had my father's Studebaker; Warren rode shotgun (front seat, passenger side) and Frankie soloed it in the back seat. The radio blared and the windows were down. We tried to catch as many red lights as possible, especially the significant ones in front of Sibleys or the four corners. There was no rush to these Sunday drives, unlike the tire-squealing, glass-packed mufflered, drag-racing cruises of Friday and Saturday nights. No, our anxiety seemed to leave us somewhat on Sundays, as the priest said it would. A "day of obligation" I think was the term he used. And cruising down Main Street, turning around in an alley near State Street, and cruising back up, we felt an obligation to slow down, collect our thoughts, and pray for a chance encounter with a fight or a girl, V-8's be damned.

With us—Warren, Frankie and me—it was always girls. We'd pull up to a light, leer out the window for a crucial few seconds, and then—fighting the instinct and good sense to shut up, we'd blurt out some trite, overused innocuous greeting, such as "Hey, what's goin' on?" or "Hey, didn't I see you at the Flyers' Club Friday night?" We were too young to go to the Flyers' Club, but that didn't matter. Speech for us was simply the grunt to affirm our adolescent presence. Communication was not crucial during the sixty seconds or so of a red light. It was all in the eyes.

Half the time we'd end our little dialogue by trying to insult the girls who wouldn't give us the time of day and who pulled away in a car we'd only dream of owning in our neighborhood. Then we'd blame it on who-ever was riding shotgun—on this day it was Warren, and we were all ready to blame it on the size of his head when we heard the lovely two girls in the car next to us say, "Why don't you follow us. . . ."

We were impressed when the "chase" led down East Avenue, over to Monroe and into a ritzy neighborhood in Brighton. I don't remember the one girl's name, the driver's, but she motioned to us to follow her into a long driveway in front of a huge Tudor home with ivy covering the stucco walls. She came over to the car as I pulled in behind them and asked if we'd like to come in for a Coke. I turned around to confer with my friends, only to see their faces brighten and eyes bulge as if, after all, they had beheld the light of the Sabbath. Actually, it was the light of her companion they beheld. Her name was Sheila and she was, without question, beautiful!

Her silky black hair hung down to her shapely waist. Her eyes were equally black, darkly ablaze above her delicately pronounced cheekbones. I don't think any of us was prepared for such a proportioned display of physical aesthetics. When she smiled at us, the whole world seemed a mere complement to her presence. Inside, we said hello to the other girl's parents and went down to a family room in the cellar where we had a Coke and listened to records. They were students at Brighton High, and to tell the truth I can't remember anything we talked about until we left about an hour later—when Sheila asked us if we'd take her home!

We looked at each other, amazed at our good fortune. Of course we had no particular scenarios in mind; to simply be in the company of such a stunning girl was a blessing we felt characteristically unworthy of. So one can imagine the shock when, sitting between Warren and me in the front seat of the Studebaker as we drove up Monroe Avenue past Cobbs Hill, she pointed and said "Why don't we go up there."

I think it's fair to say that none of us growing up in the Bay-Goodman area in the early sixties expected anything in return for simply being alive.

"Cobbs Hill . . . the reservoir?" I asked, feeling sure my imagination was playing tricks on me. It was, of course, the place where lovers went parking in Rochester. I had never parked there, and my guess was that neither Warren nor Frankie had either. After all, we were just seventeen and not very lucky or aggressive when it came to girls. We had to have our family cars home before dark.

"Yes," repeated Sheila, pushing her silky black hair aside and turning to me, "why don't we park by the reservoir."

I remember wanting to apologize for turning the car off. Warren had his arm around her and I checked the back seat to see if Frankie had passed out. He was bright-eyed, but I could tell he was as nervous as I was. I not only didn't know what to do, I didn't know what I wanted! I think it was Frankie who asked her if she liked baseball, and at that point I gave up the thought of a conversation.

I guess she kissed Warren first, and after a few minutes she began necking with me. Even Frankie leaned forward over the seat and got into the act. I don't know about the others, but I wanted to tell her things in private, like how soft her lips were, how she fit so precisely in my thin arms, or how I'd been searching for someone exactly like her. But of course I said nothing.

I think all of us were dreaming that early evening as we dropped her off on a side street off Monroe Avenue. Nobody said anything for a few minutes. Then Warren laughed. He said he wasn't sure but while he was necking with Sheila he felt her hand touch him, by chance perhaps, where he hadn't been touched much by another human being. I was astonished, because I had felt the same thing—and like Warren, I had assumed it was due to the crowded nature of the front seat. When I told the others this, we all laughed some more, thinking we might have been more naive than we realized in our romantic impressions.

But in the end we insisted on our innocence—not quite able to imagine a sexual invitation on the part of such a dark-eyed beauty. Warren admitted a couple days later that he'd been thinking about inviting her to the junior prom—and I'm admitting now that I'd had the same thoughts! But neither of us took her to the prom; as a matter of fact none of us ever saw her again. As with so many things in our lives, so many of our encounters, it was a passing moment, however bewildering.

But for us, on a Sunday afternoon so fraught with boredom, loneliness, and the need for companionship fused with beauty, it became a romantic touchstone that would color our worlds for a long time.

A few weeks later Warren laughed about it, realizing we'd never see Sheila again: "How could we be so dumb?" he asked, turning his eyes toward the unresponsive sky.

It was Frankie who spoke up—his wisdom unappreciated at the time: "It wouldn't have been the same . . ."

And he was right. Anything more than what had happened with Sheila wouldn't have lasted a week in our minds. We were Romantic Adolescents then, learning through our awkward sexual pursuits to be, in the end, Romantic Adults. Our most enduring dreams reflected, with a glamour we did not possess, our common decency.

5. TENNIS, POETRY, AND ALL THINGS
SWEATY AND BEAUTIFUL

We've been doing the solitary thing long enough.

—Coleman Barks

In 1976, while still living the life of university writer, I initiated a ten-day event that brought poets together with new kinds of audiences, all centered around the game of tennis. I did not know it at the time, but it was the first excursion of my journey into the world of poetry and common people. The fact that it was probably the "healthiest" poetry festival ever in the minds of those who participated, writers and audiences, was apparent at the time. However, it soon became clear on reflection that the event symbolized an opening for art itself. I wrote this essay the following year, and it seems appropriate to include it as part of this collection, for the trip to Arizona marked my first steps to Rochester.

A Related Note:
There is, as I imagine the reader can detect throughout this book, an inherent contradiction between moral and idealistic convictions and our individual ambitions for recognition and respect within a society of professionals, especially in artistic colonies. If I did not admit to this contradiction in myself, this book would quickly lose its credibility. The tennis episode described below offers a fine example of such a contradiction. As a young poet at the time, I was very happy to be a part of such a distinguished group—not only to receive by association respect and recognition as a poet, but to aspire to write poems as fine as Galway Kinnell's, to fill my

own writing with the intelligence and irony of Bill Matthews's work, and to be someday a perceptive, articulate educator like Marvin Bell. At the time, I was publishing my poems in every "important" literary journal across the country. I was "on my way," convinced that the soul itself required "fame." Stubbornly (but naturally), I'm sure I still hunger for such recognition, and I can't deny that. But what became apparent during the ten days in Arizona, and in my life as a poet and a public servant in the years to follow, centers on a word crucial to the creation of this book: survival.

If there is one perception, one paranoia common among poets across the country—not only young poets attempting to become members of a literary circle, but established poets as well, it is a sense of not being appreciated. *I feel it myself, of course, some days doubting my decision to not routinely send out poems and manuscripts and instead spend my time finding social outlets for poetry and language. But I can tell you it is a feeling among our best, most recognized poets as well. We generally attribute this to the "egos of artists," but we can be more specific than that. What we loved about our tennis days in Arizona was the sharing of our humanistic natures with all kinds of people. As private as the process of writing might be, it does not define our holistic identities. Our sense of* survival *comes not from a perception of "making it" (anthologized, respected, perennial guests at summer writing festivals), but as a perception of being engaged in a struggle for life itself,* a struggle in which only those organisms best adapted to existing conditions are able to survive and reproduce. *When I describe the "health" of the poets in the following essay, I'm referring to an invigorating sense of existence, not based solely on the printed word, but on a larger, more encompassing perspective based on celebrating life through language, human utterance, and attitude. We adapt to our culture as participants; what we reproduce as artists is the belief in and ability to change—both others and ourselves. . . .*

I removed my racquet cover and looked at the mysterious X in the center of the new racquet. It was a trademark, apparently, of the pro I had found the day before who would string my racquet while I waited (the old racquet breaking at such a time was surely a sign so obvious I dismissed it). The pro said it would keep the strings from spreading and would not affect the flight or spin of the ball. All I knew was that it looked odd, as if my initial were *X*, like the signature of my grandfather, or a symbol of a kiss, or death, or both! I had arrived at O'Hare airport early, by almost an hour. I wondered if anyone would guess that I was on my way to a tennis tournament. I wanted someone to ask. But no one did. This was a fantasy—a quirk that somehow turned into a reality: a legitimate tennis tournament for poets!

Two weeks earlier I'd received a call from the posh site of the tournament, the Wickenburg Inn, about an hour north of Phoenix, Arizona.

"Ross, I hate to tell you this, but the whole thing is off."

"What? What do you mean . . . " I was shocked; the student I had been talking to looked on in my office as my hand shook a little while holding the receiver (at least that's what the student said later).

"We're in receivership." The voice was that of the manager's, Ed.

"Receivership? What do you mean?"

"Ross, everything here that we do has to be okayed by the courts . . . and they're just not going to go for the tournament."

There had been difficulties all along. Poets kept dropping out: Phil Levine because of a bad shoulder; Mark Strand because of a trip; David St. John, who was the No. 1 seed, because of a "pressing engagement" (an upcoming marriage); Stanley Kunitz because of a bad disc. So substitutions had to be made, which was complicated for two reasons: two universities in Arizona, the University of Arizona in Tucson and Arizona State University in Tempe, were actually financing the trip by scheduling gala poetry festivals in which each university had to approve of and adjust to each substitution; and what had to be considered in choosing the poets was a fine balance between tennis ability and literary reputation!

Stanley Kunitz especially wanted to take part. Here was a man who played tennis with the great tennis-poets: Theodore Roethke and Randall Jarrell. He wanted to pass the tennis racquet like a torch on to the younger poets . . . a tradition. But Kunitz, who's about seventy years old, came up with a bad back; he tried everything for a quick cure, but time was short. Finally he canceled out, reluctantly. It was a pity.

Of course the key to the whole event was the tennis resort's interest in hosting the tournament. It came about by a hunch I had while reading the travel section of the *Chicago Sunday Tribune*. For a few years several poets talked about a tournament, but always it came down to a university hosting the tournament, and the details could never be worked out—because universities are not really interested in hosting tennis tournaments for poets! That Sunday, I read about a luxurious tennis resort in Arizona that offered as a sidelight arts and crafts programs for its guests. I also read that the owner was a man who lived in Chicago. The next day I called the owner and proposed a poetry program for the resort during which the poets—besides being available to guests for readings, workshops, and informal chats—would hold their tournament. He said it was a great idea!

"Ed, we can't cancel it. I don't know how many thousands of dollars the universities committed to this, and the publicity has been out for at least a couple of weeks . . . there's no way we can cancel."

"Well, let me get back to you tomorrow, Ross. I want to try and work something out. This is difficult for everyone."

When it came to literary matters, nothing had ever seemed to work out for me ("this is the best whole ms. I've ever received for the Braziller Series" reads the beginning of one rejection), except, that is, for people liking my poems, which I led myself to believe meant everything. The last flop was my first full-length book of poems, which was printed so poorly and handled so terribly that it was never distributed or reviewed. But even that was my *own* problem, one I could cope with, no matter how difficult. This, on the other hand, involved seven other poets and nine days out of each of their lives, and two huge universities and countless individuals. I was nervous; especially when one of the poets, George Keithley of California, called and said he had phoned the Wickenburg Inn and was told the reservations for the poets were canceled!

In the TWA corridor at O'Hare stood a man later described by poet Dave Smith as a "sensuous Eskimo." It was Galway Kinnell, as healthy looking and handsome as ever. He was the major poet of the group, and the oldest, fifty. I had originally seeded him third in the tournament, but he would eventually end up second, pushing himself with such determination and hard work that the tournament took on the dimension of a legitimate sporting event—and it was reported as such by a reporter from a magazine called *South Shore,* the bearded, long-haired, soft-spoken reporter (Harry Briggs) whispering into a tape recorder as he covered point by point the finals between Kinnell and Steve Dunn and the match for third place between Coleman Barks and me. Months earlier, two of the poets contacted *Sports Illustrated* to see if J. D. Reed was interested in covering the event. Neither ever received an answer. (And why should they?) I did tell George Plimpton about it, who replied, "It's just a bunch of poets playing tennis!" How true. Like a writer playing quarterback, or comedian. Or an entertainer playing celebrity. How true. Poets just playing tennis. I. A. Richards' normalcy of the poet . . . or was it the equilibrium of the athlete? Poets playing tennis. Poets writing out checks on the first of the month. Poets waxing their cars. Plimpton cracking his first joke to a half-drunk audience in Las Vegas. How true. Just a bunch of poets writing poems!

On the plane to Phoenix, Kinnell and I worked out a complicated system to determine what the doubles' combinations would be. It took about an hour to figure out and when we arrived at the lounge in the Phoenix airport, we discovered we had left the pairings on the plane. After a beer and a couple of games of electric hockey, we made out the doubles schedule once again. But as we did there was something uneasy between us.

A hoax? Kinnell and I were to be the last to arrive—at seven o'clock. We were to meet the others (a couple of poets were scheduled to arrive early in the afternoon) in the Governor's Lounge in the east terminal of the airport. It was about half past seven and not a poet to be found. We asked waitresses and checked the name of the lounge. But no poets. The van from the tennis resort was supposed to pick up the group a little after eight. Perhaps, if Kinnell and I were to walk outside, there would be nothing but desert. In a way, that seemed more real than being put up at one of the most luxurious resorts in Arizona to play tennis and read poems (which, it turned out, we didn't have to do at the resort). In the university workshops that almost all of them came out of, poets of my generation had drilled into them the notion that nobody cares about poetry. Yet it was told to them not with disappointment but with pride: it made the art pure—nothing to tempt a poet to write one way or the other—and the poet virtuous! Unfortunately, such a notion conveniently lent itself to the most powerful force in America in the sixties and seventies—the tendency toward self-absorption. So poets started writing for other poets or, even worse, for no one; editors and publishers stopped asking if anyone might like (and buy!) a book of poetry, and considered instead how their choices might impress other critics. The result: a small literary community enamored of itself and thoroughly cynical and condescending toward any reading public. It struck me that under such conditions the true lyric could not survive. Then it struck me that there was no real lyric tradition in America to speak of— Walt Whitman being perhaps the first and last lyric poet. It struck me also (a long time before) that isolation breeds a tendency toward false virtue.

So two poets, fooled by their belief that some business organization was going to welcome them to dwell in luxury for a few days, two poets alone in the desert, seemed very real. But a few minutes after eight o'clock a black beard floated through a soft-lit archway in the back of the lounge. Attached to it was a face, and under it a body that would be seen in the following days trying to balance a tennis racquet and a large brain, while displaying in a dazzling fashion a sweatshirt with the words *Last Seed* across its back. Marvin Bell led the two to a back room where the rest of the poets had been waiting for at least a couple of hours. It looked like the after-hours of a night-long poker game. Dave Smith from Utah had been there since early afternoon, spending almost all of that time in front of a television set in one of the lounges, the buzzing light of the tube turning his eyelids dark and his spine a little soft as he collapsed in a chair at the end of the table. Bill "Boogie 'til You Puke" Matthews fidgeted with a cigarette, his nervous energy a result of sleepless nights. Steve Dunn, calm and confident—he knew he would win the tournament, and he did. Even the teenage face of forty-year-old good ol' boy Coleman Barks bore a five o'clock shadow that a week later would make a faint return and follow each poet to the lectern when we read our poems. And next to him, bloodshot eyes filled with either mystic visions or bourbon, a poet I had never met. It was George Keithley, who literally, in his life and in his poetry, followed the Donner Party trail until exhausted, and, during the next few days while walking back from the net after a put-away, would hold up his racquet and tilt his head as if discovering a snowshoe long after the blizzard.

I looked at the tired, motley crew. I felt as if I should deal out the cards and close the cellar door. It was obvious no one knew what in god's name they were doing. I didn't think any one of them believed that a van from the Wickenburg Inn would be there in a few minutes to pick us up.

"You the poets going out to the Wickenburg Inn?" asked a thin, dark-haired young man with a cap that read *Wickenburg*. He helped load the heap of ancient traveling bags and suitcases and ragged-gripped tennis racquets into the back of the van. The poets got in, and joked a little with each other. But it was evident. We did not know where we were going.

Eight poets in a van staring out into the black night trying to conjure up some image of the desert they are traveling through, baffled not by geography or purpose but by welcome, respect, and something unnamable, religious in nature, like an atheist's synonym for faith. We talked about Roethke, the grand tennis-poet, and of a tournament in his name. We made excuses for our conditions, and I wondered if a good game of tennis had anything to do with the elements that made a good poem. A few days later Coleman Barks would describe my tennis game with a poetic tinge: "Your concentration fluctuates from point to point; one moment you have a sword, the next a strand of spaghetti."

"Look," I laughed as they pulled into the town of Wickenburg and he pointed to a huge neon sign ablaze in the black Arizona sky, "an Italian restaurant!"

But no one laughed.

"I guess that's not funny." I apologized, my Italian name no more than a label under a poem, certainly not a link to a heritage . . .

Then they laughed.

I would make others laugh during the trip—audiences too. In Tucson about a week later, I would make the huge audience of three hundred or so laugh plenty, eliciting giggles even during my most serious poems. I was furious at myself. A day earlier I had given a splendid reading at Tempe. But in Tucson the two characters of a poetry reading—entertainer and the writer of poems—interfered with each other, the entertainer once again getting the upper hand: poet as personality, the Romantic curiosity distorted by the American fascination with "type." What kind of a man writes poetry? What kind of a man reads *Playboy?* And at a reading a poet steps out from the isolation of his room, steps out from the isolation and desolation of being a "maker" without a product (books don't sell?), and steps onto a stage and desires a reaction from an audience—and humor elicits the most obvious response, each laughter a chorus of "I like you's." And I was always a good storyteller— but my poems are serious and passionate. *One moment spaghetti, another moment a sword.*

Once word of the tennis tournament got around I received several "friendly" notes from other poets. I felt like an editor of a magazine or a new poetry publication series. I hated the politics of such situations, the petty bickering, jealousy, and ill feelings that seem to permeate the literary community. Of course artists without audiences tend to grope toward each other and foster the political atmosphere. I remembered once trying to be convinced by Ted Solotaroff and Len Fulton that it was healthy for poets to get involved in the whole publishing business. I felt, on the other hand, it was destructive to some poets—especially those weak enough to be enticed into giving too much energy to business instead of poetry; and some of those weak poets might be our best— their vulnerability to be expressed and transformed into art, not to be tested like a car bumper. But, I had to admit, the politicians prevailed, ironically thriving with the absence of audience, the reading public, who could be convinced not only that it possessed no critical faculties for poetry but that it had no taste whatsoever. How subconsciously clever. The supreme achievement of the technological state: to convince its citizens that they have no taste!

Ten miles or so outside of Wickenburg the van turned down a dirt road. We noticed a few faint lights (which turned out to be gas lamps) and some small hills. When we reached the lodge, a rustic-looking structure made out of logs and adobe brick, we got out and tried to take in what we could—the pure air, the clear stars. We bunched in a group, like kids in a strange place.

In the black quiet of the desert night eight poets transferred their scrappy luggage and tennis racquets to three electric carts. A moment before we were a little relieved when the woman at the registration desk acknowledged our arrival and had us sign "Poets' Group" after the line on the white card that said *type of payment*. But our curiosity still rendered us quiet. Packed with luggage and men, each cart made its way to and up a group of hills where the adobe cottages stood. The little lights on each cart were so faint that they seemed to enhance the darkness more than anything else. The poets didn't speak. The air was neither warm nor cold, just something to exist in. The electric motor strained as the cart made its way up, and we slowed almost to a stop— but there wasn't any worry, just a bunch of eyes testing their powers in the darkness. In the van on the way to the resort, some of us had joked about being taken away forever, and now that thought crossed my mind—but in a different way. The cottages were lovely, as much as I could make out; and when Dave Smith and Coleman Barks got off, picked up their bags and opened the door of their casita, I glanced inside and saw the fireplace, the arched stone bookshelves, the log-beam ceilings, the leather easy chair—and the bottle of wine waiting, two gleaming glasses on either side. I glanced at the two poets' faces, and at the incredible clarity of the stars above, and sniffed the wonderful air that surely would enter wholly and freely into the complex loveliness of breath. Taken away forever? The poets had had in mind a prison when they joked. I glanced over my shoulder and saw the moonlight falling over the tennis courts at the edge of the slope of this desert landscape. The eerie sound of the cart seemed to give life a purpose, a direction. Kinnell and I sat on the back of the cart not saying anything. What could we say—"It's beautiful"? It *was* beautiful, too beautiful. The rancher stopped the cart at the porch of another adobe. Even the sand seemed to apologize for all the difficult steps one takes in a lifetime. We went in—there were the wine and glasses, and apples and oranges, and a handwritten note of welcome from the manager. And in the bedroom, toffee and candy kisses on the pillows. The cart drove off in the same silence. Two poets looked at each other, all over the world. We had been taken away, given a perfect climate, three incredible meals a day, all the tennis one wanted, a horse to ride, clean sheets to sleep in, and clean towels that would appear mysteriously three or four times a day (giving a few of the poets momentary complexes). The manager said "Anything you need, just ask," and there were candy kisses on pillows each night. And guests who came over because they had never spoken to a poet before, and the gentleman in charge of food service who sat down and told his dreams. We had been taken away—the silent cart making its way through the sandy black night, the adobe huts looking more like a movie set. The younger poet and the older poet walked down under the moonlight onto the courts and touched the nets.

On the campus of Arizona State University, on a Monday afternoon, seven men got out of a van, picked up their suitcases and tennis racquets and made their way across the quad. Too old and too varying in size . . . anyone who saw them knew this wasn't the tennis team. The night before, after dinner at the resort, over a drink or two (but never more), the poets—aged from thirty-two to fifty, I being the youngest, Kinnell the oldest—agreed that they had never felt healthier. They had played anywhere from six to ten sets of tennis a day, had ridden horses, hiked through the desert, had eaten three splendid, nourishing meals a day, and had slept as soundly as the muse during the filing of income taxes. They had meant physically healthier, of course, the body catching up to the mind. But it was more than that.

On the night of the cookout, only two of us rode horses to the campsite, about an hour away—Kinnell and me (the others got there via hayride). It was the first time Galway had been on a horse. He tried to keep his horse at a slow and steady walk. Perhaps that was the pace of the poem he was thinking. I knew how to ride, galloped, trotted, and waited for my friend to catch up. He and the horse would appear at precisely the same pace, poet and hoofbeat in some gentle check on the value and ease of domestication.

When we arrived at the cookout, night had fallen; the fires were raging, and the others were waiting with beers in hand. It could have been a Michelob commercial, but there wasn't any Michelob—and no one seemed to care less. During dinner, wonderful steaks and potatoes and such, the poets met more guests. The word had gotten around that there were poets at the ranch; when any of the poets introduced themselves, there were the usual responses—"Oh, so you're the one. . . ." Yet there were no romantic sighs, no brows lowered in suspicion of faggots or weirdos, no recitings of Longfellow. The guests—during the entire stay—treated us the way we hoped our poems would be read—*civilly,* with curiosity and respect. They asked questions, basic ones—like what we did—because they didn't really know what poetry is, let alone what a poet might be. They told us some things about themselves, dreams, unusual events they deemed meaningful, etc.—because *down deep they did know about poetry* and the need to communicate. And they never overwhelmed us, but treated us decently. Why? Because we *listened.* We did not read poems at the ranch, or look at any, or talk about style or the quirks of personal writing habits. We listened. And we looked the guests in the eye until we saw ourselves, or our opponents the next day, when we continued our tournament and had to negotiate with the immediacy of the ball hitting the racquet (though any pro will tell you you can't see it hit). What was happening, I realized, during those happy, healthy days at the resort, was that the poet receded to his proper place in that inadequate room of self-identity, and the man stepped forward, becoming fully aware that it wasn't tennis that was vital, of course, but it wasn't poetry either! It was being decent, hard living, hard playing, sensitive, patient, intelligent, respectful, etc., etc.   all those things that come from interaction as well as isolation. I saw in these poets the qualities that gave them a normality so incredible and definitive that their poems became the only badges worthy of their decoration. At the end of the evening a few cowhands sang and played guitars, and before long everyone, including us, was singing along to "Up against the wall, Redneck Mother." The song didn't matter—it just happened to be the one most apt to the occasion—it was the celebration that was essential. We sang and the fire blazed because for the moment that was our only place on this earth. Later, when I was riding my horse back and I became separated from the rest in the dark desert under the big moon, I kicked my heels and the horse kicked its heels and we galloped off into the night—I felt any destination was fine on such a beautiful night. But the horse headed straight for the stable, hungry and tired.

The next day Dave Smith bandaged up his thumb, his fingers, his feet . . . he hadn't been playing much tennis and had exhausted himself and bits of his flesh during the long hours of the tournament. What impressed me was that Dave's game kept getting better, as if his exhaustion were some skin to be shed, which would allow exposure of some inner strength. In the finals of the consolation doubles event, he and I won easily, and the poet from Utah played impressively. What obligation Dave Smith had to himself, I didn't know; but I was sure that such an obligation could not be separated from the one the calloused, bandaged, sore-muscled poet felt to his tennis friends. A small example of courage and determination, perhaps, or in Plimpton's words, just a tennis game. But to me, that strength symbolized the bonds these poets were making between themselves; more than that, the bond between our concepts of ourselves as exceptional (poets) and our concepts of ourselves as ordinary (tennis players, etc.). As the concepts merge, they strengthen, reinforce each other—in effect, the ego was being neutralized. The worn-out, sweaty, hard-breathing, limping poets would not intimidate any of the guests, even if the subject of poetry were brought up. And yet, the respect for, the acceptance of these artists grew in just four days—to the point where we were being asked to come back!

It would have been a holiday for I. A. Richards, pointing out the "ordinary" backhand of Marvin Bell, the "common" overhead of Bill Matthews, the "usual" foot fault of my own weak serve. And it didn't take a videotape for the poets to see themselves, as Richards suggests, as normal human beings. At a time when the poet as personality ranks higher than the poet as writer of poems, eight poets were discovering something common and vital between themselves and others. It didn't have to be tennis, but that was the catalyst this time that allowed us to release ourselves from an identity based on stereotype, myth, and general misunderstanding. Eccentricity didn't distinguish this group—nor did jealousy, paranoia, or pettiness. Interestingly, at least two poets (and, readers, you'd be surprised who) expressed a desire to write articles comparing the poets' poetry with their tennis games—the distinguished style with the half-assed strategy. I looked forward to such attempts, realizing what the Greeks and their descendants realized—that art stands out, becomes distinctive, when it avails itself more readily to a public who anticipates art and excellence from within the framework of a character familiar and, apart from the creative impulse, ordinary in nature.

And on that last night on the ranch we agreed we had never felt healthier . . .

But of course poets get the itch to go off by themselves, explore, think it over, write it down. After a tennis match one morning, Coleman Barks went off into the desert with a book. When I saw him later, Coleman said he apparently left the book somewhere in the desert. Today, when I think of the warm embraces the poets gave each other the night before we left at a party in Tucson, I think of that book, the easy desert wind blowing the pages open, and the Arizona sun burning upon the print, and Coleman's footprints disappearing deeper under the sand as we move from isolation and surfaces toward the center of the earth.

Our children gone . . . that's what Christmas means to me now," says Jean, in her seventies, when asked what the holiday means to her. Several other senior citizen writers in our group make similar comments about feeling "alone" at a time they should be experiencing joy. "It's a big country," adds Bob, jotting down a few notes, "you've got to learn how to live alone."

Every year, come October, both our senior citizen and youth writing workshops begin to create group poems that will appear as the inside lyrics to original "seasons' greetings" cards from each of our recreation centers. Once the poem is completed and we find someone to illustrate the front of the card with an original drawing, we print them ourselves in our duplicating center in the basement of City Hall and hand out hundreds of them with envelopes to senior citizen and youth participants in the program. Sometimes the newspapers print one or two of them in a human-interest column on Christmas Day.

There are two processes that reveal themselves during the "greeting card" workshops. The first, of course, is how a poem gets written. The group poem allows me to take the lead and examine the process of how random images and thoughts can be connected, considered, disassociated, and eventually molded into focus. It is important for the workshop participants to see the revising and editing of a single work as it occurs spontaneously. The dialogue we encounter as members of the workshop read off their random phrases and we discuss them reflects the mental dialogue each writer endures during the creative act. It is important to see the process of elimination, particularly of the clichés and generalities, as the poem slowly takes its form. The fact that each poem will contain phrases from individual participants makes the experience more meaningful, especially when the final product is seen, signed, and sent off to someone less than two months after the initial meeting.

And that is the second process—to see the connection between the chance utterance and the completed expression—to see the urge to communicate something not yet articulated turn into not just a group of printed words, but a true celebration of a moment, which is surely the intent of a greeting card—as well as the intent of literature. For most people, that is a process never revealed.

But it is also the intent of those producing literature to be original, to give language its power of renewal, and to create insight and a fuller awareness of the surrounding world. So I probe, a true devil's advocate, a persistent angel with both feet in the mud. The writer, it becomes clear, is a combination detective/psychologist/balladeer. We list the random images—*icicles hanging from eaves, a shovel imbedded in a snowdrift, gifts torn open under the tree.* We make another list of thoughts—*image without substance, holidays are not for everyone, every lonely person is at the center of the universe.* Along the way we dismiss several clichés—an integral part of the process becomes very evident: to get rid of the inevitable trash, the language experience. "Get more physical," I hear myself saying again. It seems I keep redefining "ambiguity" every ten minutes, trying to get people comfortable with the idea of entertaining two emotions at once.

The kids at one recreation center eventually choose a topic for their card—a bum they see often in the neighborhood. *The snowflakes fall onto the dumpster . . .* their poem begins, and already the worlds of spirit and reality begin to merge. The bum's name, believe it or not, is *Santos*—and I'm quick to point out, and define, the ironies of life that surround us. They follow the exercise and supply the physical setting— Santos the bum asleep on a bench on a particular street beside the glass-enclosed bus stop. I lead them on with a simple question—what do you do when you sleep?

> He must dream too
>> on Christmas Eve, maybe of socks,
>> or ear muffs, or a beautiful
>>> red wool scarf,
> things that will make him warm.
> Maybe he will dream that the other Santa
>> will make him young again . . .

They complete the poem with another stark fact: that they, no matter what their wishes for the old man, haven't any money to give him. So they give him what they can—thus discovering the spirit of the season:

> If I had a buck or a dream,
>> I'd give it to him.
> But I give him my sympathy instead.

The senior citizens of another writing group give me some straightforward terms to describe their thoughts for the holiday season—"no jobs" and "3% interest in the bank." Our discussion of those terms brings us to the question of comparison—to other times, other feelings about Christmas through the years. And as the images begin to emerge, the spirit begins to flow, and by the end of the poem, we've gone from anxiety over finances to a rediscovery of hope.

Song of the Holiday, Old and Young

No jobs.
3% interest at the bank.
Good meals at the nutrition center,
nothing much in the cupboard.
Still, the snow falls,
big, feathery flakes that touch
your eyelids like a dream.
A child laces his skates;
his eyes fill with innocence and freedom.

He has no destination.
Bells echo through the streets,
a burley man blows in his hands,
there's still a lot of room
in the kettle,
not enough dropping their change
this year, but some do.
At midnight
the carolers converge from
every neighborhood, their voices
off-key but beautiful.
We are all children,
waiting for a surprise in the morning.

Another group of kids chooses a different subject for their holiday poem—one very much in their minds. An acquaintance of theirs had been beaten and killed just a few weeks earlier, and I assure them their feelings might indeed be very appropriate as an expression of the season's message.

SEASONS GREETINGS AND GOODBYES
for Mark Renod Dixon
(June 10, 1972–October 5, 1991)

Snowflakes fall on the empty space
on his porch on Hudson Avenue,
where he sat watching the anger
build on the streets.
Snowdrifts as high as castles,
Stars shine like broken glass . . .
Mark's eyes seemed to glisten,
maybe because he needed glasses,
maybe because he wanted to see
a world without violence, the soft
crystal sand of West Palm Beach
where he was born, the blue ocean

with its slow, peaceful waves . . .
But there are no gifts for Mark
this year. He was beat up
on a Saturday afternoon in the
October sun that warmed his
last breath . . . No gloves to keep his
hands from becoming fists,
no sneakers so he could run away
from those dudes.
I wish we could have given him,
at least, eye glasses, so he could see
the snowflakes turning to sand, there,
in West Palm Beach, where he is
just a boy again, hoping
to live a long life.

In our oral history workshop at our residence for elderly blacks, Maimie Lee Haynes, almost eighty years old, told a story that began as a variation of the "Coal Story." But our patience as listeners gave her the time and reflection necessary for the gist of the story to emerge—and hers, in the true holiday spirit, transformed itself into one of love, hardship, and finally the incredible initiation of mutual respect between daughter and mother. Her poem, along with a biographical sketch, was printed by the local newspaper on Christmas Eve. It was so well received that the well-known artist Ramon Santiago volunteered to do the drawing for the front of the city Christmas card we produced. Today it is a collector's item.

THE GIFT
story by Mamie Lee Haynes
(transcribed and written by Ross Talarico)
Bainbridge, Georgia, 1926

We kept wonderin' why he didn't come
every year.
And Ma would say, well, the yard's a mess
and Santa don't like no messy yard

to park his sleigh in.
So that year we swept the dirt yard,
cleaned the hen coop daily, crawled
under the house and pulled out the
garbage,
picked up the leaves, and even
painted the front gate with whitewash.
On Christmas morning we found pieces of
broken glass in our fireplace.
Ma said, well, I guess he broke his toys
when he landed, and left.
Turns out, though, we didn't find out
'til some years later, Ma broke up some old
crystal glass in the fireplace.

So that next year, we swept and cleaned
and picked up the yard even harder.
But my hopes were fadin'
being the oldest of our bunch (Ma would
have 13 of us in all!)
so I started gatherin' some sticks and
tall grasses, and some material my Ma
and her friends who sewed for the white folk
had around.
I tied the grass together, making a ball of it
for the head, rolling the hair, and covering
the dolls with beautiful dresses of
gingham, pongee, or linen or whatever I
could get a hold of and sew together.

And that Christmas
I had a doll for every one of
my brothers and sisters.
But when I got up early to put them
out by the fireplace that morning, expecting
nothing but maybe some pieces of broken
glass,

I saw the most beautiful basket of apples,
oranges and nuts I had ever seen.
My Ma looked at me
and I looked at her
while my brothers and sisters held their
dolls
and touched the fruit in the basket.
I was only 10 or so,
but I understood, and so did she,
the gift we had together:
Santa had come to our house.

And one other. Darlene Bargmann's story was also published in the newspaper, *The Democrat and Chronicle*, on Christmas Day.

SILVER DOLLARS, SILVER MEMORIES
story by Darlene Bargmann
(transcribed and written by Ross Talarico)

Every year when my mother had a child,
my father gave her a silver dollar. So she
had eight silver dollars. Can you believe
that my entire childhood was spent
borrowing these silver dollars and getting
them back . . .

My mother was born in 1889 in Montana.
My father was born ten years earlier than
that in Michigan, and somehow made his
way to Butte, Montana and married my
mother. But there was no work in
Montana, so my father went off to find
work. "Go anyplace and I'll follow—
anyplace but New York City," my mother
said to my father as he left. So I'm here to
tell you that he went right to New York
City and found work as a barber!

Mom arrived with us to a cold water flat in Brooklyn. There was plumbing, but no hot water—just a coal stove in the kitchen where you could heat up water in the back. The tenement houses were usually about six stories high—and since the farther up the less expensive the flats, I want to tell you that we always lived on the top floor.

No, my mom didn't like it, but she knew she'd never have enough money to move back to Montana, so she said if she had to stay there, she'd make it the best life she could. And she did. Those were the days of large families, the days when moms were home. I remember how happy I was to climb the stairs past the floors of all the families—especially in the afternoons when all the cooking was being done. I can still remember the aroma of the pasta from the Italian family on the second floor, and the German sauerkraut on the third floor, and the sausage from the Polish family under us. We got along and there was a warm feeling of belonging that we all shared.

On the top floor, our flat, everyone crowded in on Saturday nights. We were not, let me tell you, a quiet family. My father played the mandolin, my brother Bob the guitar, Billy the banjo, and my brother Lou the saxophone. They would play and everyone would keep rhythm and sing along. I remember my mother putting pillows under our feet as we kept to the music, trying to keep the noise down. But there were times when neighbors tapped broom handles on the ceiling to complain. Funny, we didn't have much, but we were a together family, a loving family.

No, my mother would never get back to Montana, but she left me the most wonderful inheritance I believe possible to bequeath a child—because she knew how to love, how to make you feel so good. She knew how to mother children—and I've certainly put that to good use in my life.

I was the last born, in 1930. I was the eighth silver dollar. My mother had a can, a coffee or cocoa can I believe. She didn't believe in banks (and we had nothing to keep in a bank!). And she'd hammer this can into the floor of the closet wherever we lived (and we moved often, let me tell you). In that can she kept the silver dollars my father gave her for each child that was born. I don't know how she thought that would keep the silver dollars from being stolen, but that was her idea. They were her prized possessions.

All of us knew how important these silver dollars were to her. She'd get out an old rag and polish them and then start to tell the stories behind them—who was there when the child was born, what the times were like, what the weather had been, if the child were early or late . . . I can't tell you the times mama and papa took out those silver dollars and the stories that would unfold when they began talking about them. As a matter of fact, the stories seemed to grow as the years went by—more and more details emerged; so I guess they were storytellers after all, just like I am now.

We were our own bank. We felt somehow we were rich with our silver dollars—*eight* silver dollars! When times would get rough, we'd take a silver dollar out of our "bank," the can in the closet, and we'd buy some groceries and tell the grocery man to save the silver dollar and we'd buy it back. I can't tell you how many times we bought back those silver dollars!

Now I'll tell you one story about those silver dollars. It was December. I was born in the middle of the depression, and I was about four or five, so it must have been around 1934. We had no money, and like others were having a tough time financially. My mother made many things we needed to live, including gifts for Christmas. But we were very poor that year.

So we took a silver dollar to the grocery store and asked him to hold it and we'd buy it back. He was a jolly old Italian man with a mustache and a big white apron and a straw hat, and he always did this willingly. In those times grocers and others had to create their own systems of credit and trust so everyone could survive. That was early December. We had another silver dollar out at the same time —with the man who sold the bags of coal we needed to warm the flat.

On my way home from school one day, the grocer stopped me and said that if my mama wanted that silver dollar, she'd better get me the money right away— "causa I a canta hold onto it mucha longer," he said in his thick Italian accent.

We took odd jobs and tried everything to earn money to buy back that silver dollar. We did manage to buy back the one from the coal man because we needed another bag of coal that cold December. But there was still this one silver dollar out. My mama said maybe we just had to let it go because she wanted us to have a little something for Christmas (she had been sewing for days).

My mother, by the way, was the woman people called to help them when a baby was about to be born. She was popular because she had a hand-held scale. So if you didn't have mama there when you had your baby, you wouldn't know how much your baby weighed. You'd have to wrap up your baby and go to the grocery store. So mama was immensely popular. That December, the Italian family in the building called mama. They were a nice family, fun and warm, and of course didn't have much to give, like us.

Meanwhile, we thought we had lost that silver dollar, and it was ruining our holiday.

Everytime I walked past the grocery store my heart was in my feet cause I felt so awful. It was December 24th, Christmas Eve, and I'll never forget this. The Italian man whose baby my mother helped deliver gave my mother a box of chocolate cherries, and on the top of the box was a dollar bill!

Well, let me tell you, several of my brothers and sisters took that folded dollar bill and ran to the grocery store. The man was just about to close. When we walked in with the dollar bill he was so happy to see us and gave us that silver dollar. And I'll never forget this: he wouldn't take the folding money, the dollar bill, and he handed it back to us and said, "Merry Christmas children."

Time went on, and our family prospered, but my mother always had those silver dollars. As she got older, they meant a great deal to her. When she went into a nursing home, she had to take them with her, and sad to say, I visited her one day and someone had stolen five of her silver dollars. It was, oh my, such a terrible feeling.

I bought five silver dollars and replaced them in the nursing home, and my mother never knew they were missing. But I did take the ones that she still had from my father, and took the three coins to a jeweler and now have a beautiful long necklace with the three remaining silver dollars. But I certainly have those wonderful silver memories of my wonderful parents, and those stories they wove into my childhood that can never be lost and never be stolen—because they're a great inheritance.

*F*rom the Minneapolis-St. Paul airport, we made our way to Duluth by Greyhound bus. In Duluth we were told we'd have to take a local bus into Superior.

I believe we had four suitcases, not to mention a couple of cloth handbags filled with books, fruit, shoes, and odds and ends. It was a little later than we had planned to arrive, dusk now settling amidst the huge granaries on either side of the bridge that spanned the waters of the Lake Superior channel. We had never been in Wisconsin before, or in the Midwest, or anywhere really. The dim, abandoned buildings of Superior gave me a strange feeling—as if I were entering a place and time that was assuredly a part of the past. I understood that the population of Superior had been declining since the turn of the century. We passed an old rundown bar and on the window there was a sign that read 5-cent drafts.

I squeezed June's hand, trying to comfort myself. June managed to smile at me assuredly, and even then I began to see the incredible strength of character that would allow her to endure the almost twenty years with me that followed that night.

It was our honeymoon. Our first days as husband and wife, and I was in Superior to begin my life as a college student in Wisconsin. I had no idea what lay ahead for me, for June, for America the beautiful. But getting off the bus on Superior Boulevard and standing on a deserted street corner across from the university with four suitcases, a wife, and about three hundred dollars, I just wanted to close my eyes and wish myself home. But we stood there in the deep Canadian twilight chill, the early darkness surrounding us like a great shawl, our arms around each other's waists and the streetlamp above us flickering with the first dim light of a thousand evenings.

The motel on the corner had a room, and however dingy it was, we collapsed on the old mattress and held each other. I remember thinking how quickly romance turns to anxiety, how quickly love in America turns to the instinctive urge to simply survive. I remember holding on *as our credo, not making love—and to this day I still make love in order to hold on dearly and securely.*

The next day, after I registered at the college for my courses, we called for apartments and found none available. We were told we could get a temporary apartment at the Hotel Superior, so we hauled our suitcases the ten blocks to the hotel and settled in a room with a tiny kitchenette and a Murphy bed. For us, it was a place to stay while we tried to get a grip on what in god's name we were doing there at age twenty or so and supposedly beginning a new life together.

Actually, we weren't even married, though we told everyone we were. We had taken off on a motorcycle, a few friends gathering to snap some photos and send along with us their well wishes. I look back at the photos now—my green-and-white, Triumph 500 motorcycle laden with the homemade, taped-up saddlebags, the army-surplus backpack strapped to June, and both of us waving, goodbye, hello, goodbye, hello. We made our way to a lodge on a quiet lake in the Catskills, where we had to get special permission to arrive on the grounds by motorcycle. The place was filled with older people who dressed well and seemed to celebrate every other hour with a tall cocktail of some kind served with a slice of lime in a frosted glass. I remember how quaint we seemed to a group that had gathered for drinks across the corridor from our room. They toasted us with scotch and we sipped our drinks quietly and with bewildered appreciation before making our way to our room and tossing the scotch down the toilet.

No, we weren't married. We didn't stop off at a justice of the peace like we said in Owego, New York—though we had some stranger snap our photo in front of the town hall. In order to collect ninety dollars a month from the government as a college student (since my father had died a year earlier), I couldn't be married, and we couldn't do without that money! We were, as best we could define it, in love, and we felt we couldn't be apart from each other, so we made up our marriage vows, went on our honeymoon, and returned to a dinner party thrown by relatives and friends who showered us with a few wedding gifts.

June thought she was pregnant at the time. Some nights we pulled down the Murphy bed and wept quietly in each other's embraces. Neither of us wanted a baby. Late at night, sitting under a dim light above the tiny sink in the six-by-four kitchenette, I wrote bad poetry filled with images of love and sorrow while June slept nervously in the Murphy bed.

One night I pushed the notebooks aside, the words no longer invitations to insights, but strange echoes that seemed to be coming from a place I did not want to be. So I settled next to June who was almost asleep, and I whispered what I'm sure were clichés about love and need and I held her until we awakened into the sexual clutches we knew so well.

Earlier that evening a friend of June's, an elderly woman who worked with her at the hospital, invited us to go for a drive on a scenic ridge road that overlooked Duluth. When she picked us up, I had a splitting headache and a nauseous stomach and did not want to go. June convinced me that I'd feel better in the early evening air, but when we parked by the stone overlook, the city below with its lights glimmering, I vomited over the edge. June and the woman seemed embarrassed, but I felt a strange relief. By the time we returned to our hotel apartment, my headache was gone.

And two hours later we were making love. But in the midst of it, I saw tears in June's eyes. I felt the same tears running down from my own eyes as I knelt above her. Then, in some primitive, instinctive gesture I don't quite understand to this day, I began to hit her stomach softly with my fists. One, two, one, two—I hit her with the slow, methodical rhythm of a boxer warming up to a punching bag. Surprisingly, she invited me to do so, and I continued to strike her, not hard or violently, but with the strange intensity that arises between love and frustration.

The next evening June began bleeding. I remember her smiling radiantly before we both burst into tears. The blood flowed and we could feel the muscles in our shoulders loosen. We closed our eyes and lay still and let ourselves drift for a while down the sudden current of our relief.

June left the following year and went back to a college in our hometown in upstate New York. She continued with her nursing degree and her music, her status still "a married woman," her letters factual accounts of a day-to-day life which seemed to steady the dream world I began to nurture.

Alone in Wisconsin, I studied hard, made the dean's list, and began publishing poetry in The Atlantic, The Nation, Poetry, *and elsewhere. Some people said the poems were beautiful, and late at night I would recite them to myself with a voice I had formerly reserved for prayer. But I just wrote them as they came, knowing that if I didn't take the time to write them out, they too would disappear, like so many chance possessions in our lives.*

W e live in a world of brief engagements. We wait, as market researchers know too well, for the sudden stimuli, the impulse, the quick response. Then we retreat to those long periods of passive existence which are, it could be argued, the backbone of middle class comfort in America.

Coleridge, in his discourse on poetry and the imagination, described the creative process by comparing it to the movements of a water bug: the quick spurt forward, the collective subconscious transformed into the energetic creative will, and then long periods of reflection as the bug collects its resources from its new and temporary environment.

In America, we are encouraged daily to make the quick spurt—through words, music, and visual stimuli, an intense campaign designed for a 15- to 45-second bombardment of the senses—we are encouraged to engage in our culture's new interpretation of the ultimate "creative act" in a consumer environment: *to purchase!* Our periods of reflection too have become what advertisers hope to manufacture: a pining for material goods, a daydream of accumulating those goods that represent a successful existence.

It is, in effect, a new kind of poetry we are experiencing as we come to the close of the twentieth century. It is not a poetry of enlightenment—for it is not insight nor the discovery of inner resources that entices us; it is, rather, a poetry of confirmation. We want to know—ironically now more than ever—who we are and what we require to fulfill ourselves. But the formula has changed. It is an outward, not an inward exploration. And, therefore, we never get beneath the surface. The result is a fascination with appearance rather than self-knowledge.

And yet the lingual strategies we use are quite similar in form and purpose—the abbreviated line, the striking image, the intensified moment, the musical tone that duplicates with proper variation the human utterance. If I were to flip through the pages of a *Newsweek* magazine (as I'm doing now in the midst of writing this paragraph), here are the "lines" I come across while scanning the ads, this one for Cross Pens:

> Wise Men Still
> Bear Gifts of Gold

The historical reference—the immaculate conception and the playful application of the term "wise men"—transforms the image of the gold pen into something wondrous, so in seven well-chosen words, the giving of a pen merges with the application of a miracle.

And on the next page of *Newsweek,* in an ad for Minolta cameras:

> A Camera With
> A Mind of Its Own

A line right out of a writers workshop at the University of Iowa! How elegant in its poetic technique: infusing an object with a human quality—a form of personification, so basic and universal. But this phrase is even more interesting because the image it creates also suggests, paradoxically, individuality: the person who is responsive to an ad aimed at millions will possess, like the camera, a mind of his or her own. All this in eight words, a couplet with fewer syllables than a haiku!

And on the next page of *Newsweek,* another ad with one more carefully chosen phrase, from Hyatt Legal Services:

> We've taken the fear out of legal services, around the country, and in your neighborhood.

This is a musical invitation to trust one of America's most cynical, suspicious groups of professionals: *lawyers.* It utilizes a common literary device: the juxtaposition of tone and subject matter. In this couplet we are assured that our fear will dissipate in the face of both corporate professionalism ("around the country") and hometown intimacy ("and in your neighborhood"). It's almost as effective as the phrase permanently echoing in the subconscious of many: "You're in good hands with Allstate"—a phrase that is more effective because it utilizes, as good poetry does, the universal image.

But these individual lines, unlike literature, exist in the vacuum of a simplistic motive: to create material need. They have nothing to do with the fundamental nature of literature—to establish through insight and discovery an affirmation of life itself. No, it is not enough to simply utilize the elements of poetry and literature for a marketing strategy. Something else must exist if we are to be enriched by this bombardment of language: *context*.

Poetry is, ironically, the perfect *context* for today's sound bite—a context that, given intelligence, reflection, and sincere exploration, will give the imaginative phrase texture, depth, and meaning. It can be brief but fulfilling. It has a representational nature—symbol and metaphor are the vehicles to isolate a moment and enlarge the encompassment. It is musical yet literate, whimsical yet substantial. Poetry can be, in fact, by its nature, the most satisfying means of bringing together the diverse needs of the American character: the conscious need for immediate response (the strong image, the simple musical phrase, the instant merger of the familiar and the unique), and the subconscious need to find meaning somewhere amidst the bombardment of images and words— the need to identify context.

The task—and even here I tap into the sound bite—is to bring poetry back home to Americans. What I mean by that, of course, following the earlier observations and remarks in this book, is to take the language of poetry out of the elitist hands of academics and literary isolationists, and make it accessible—without compromise—to the general public once again.

To accomplish this, we first have to see the process of creative writing—indeed, to experience it firsthand through effective workshops throughout the community. People in this country are hungry for active participation in a process. That's why it's been my contention all along that writing is the gateway to reading, rather than the other way around, as commonly seen by educators. The unique self-expression illuminates the nature of literature on a personal level. A piece of good writing creates its own readership.

That was the case with *Rochester Voices.* Suddenly, through a process that began with word games—individual phrases and spontaneous sparks of the imagination—we moved to refinement through recreational workshops, to forums and the distribution of printed materials, to book form and the subject matter of school children and the community at large. Context, in this case, was not limited to the nurturing of individual literary efforts, but extended to the interests and needs of the general public. The authors were indistinguishable from the readers. The experience of literature, it becomes clear, is derived from the experiences close at hand—from voices at once familiar and yet distinctive. The respect for the author comes back to the reader and the reader's own identity, because that identity is so closely tied to the writer's own self.

When I turn the pages of *Rochester Voices: Uncommon Writings from Common People,* I discover again the simple yet sincere process that transforms uncertainty and curiosity into pride and accomplishment. If I'm looking for literature to cite as an example of catchy lines finding their proper context, I need go no further than this book.

"I know what's mine and what isn't mine," writes thirteen-year-old Hallina Humphries in a poem about trying to find the connection between heart and mind. In her contemplative journey, as "blood drips, but I see nothing damaged," she comes to the insight that possession of feelings represents not only a claim but a burden, one she readily accepts as she concludes, "my heart and my pain belong to me." It is a poem about the depth of attaining self-identity. It comes not from a commercialized pronouncement, but from a brief encounter with reflection and imagination. It is not a "kid's poem," it is literature.

Twelve-year-old Luis Davilla writes a love poem that concludes

> Your blues eyes sparkled like
> a beautiful waterfall.

Now it's all fog.
I can't see you anymore.

And in the midst of his fifteen-minute creation, he comes to the lines
that form the core of his poem, the literary "sound bite" that has found
its context:

The only way to express myself
is inwards . . .

There is, in fact, an ageless quality that can be identified with literature. A few pages over from the poetry of youngsters, I come across
eighty-year-old Joe Pohl's poem about the memory of fishing with his
father:

The water, over the tumbled rocks,
Gurgled with that unique sound of
all shallow streams,
A sound as ancient as the earth.
We too, as fishermen, were of this
brotherhood of ancient things.

We assembled our rods, strung the lines
through the guides, attached
the lures, and stepped into the water.

"I'll go up as far as the bridge" said my father
and smiled, because he would beat me
to the first cast.
And I saw the years fall from his shoulders.

There was no gap between us now.
We were both the same age.

One could take the last two lines here, I imagine, and give them to an
ad agency to surround that particular "sound bite" with some music
and imagery, perhaps shoot it with fuzzy-filtered, black-and-white film
to suggest age, and to sell nostalgia as well as the product. Pohl, on the
other hand, this elderly man with an obvious love for language, gives
himself to his memory, dipping into it in order to discover the essence

of companionship between a boy and his dad. Someone sharing this poem needs nothing more than this musical rendering of the experience as a reminder of an ageless quality that solidifies certain relationships. There's an inner peace here—the context for each of the striking lines. Language is completely adequate here; an ad agency would have to strip this poem in order to use it for commercial purposes.

Margaret Piacentini, in her late seventies when we met, was the first senior citizen to sign up for the writers workshop when the program started in 1985. She blossomed like a teenager, her writing improving with each effort. I turn a page and there's one of her prose pieces, her voice and experience still alive in this book, though she's been dead now for more than two years. She writes about her father and the poverty of growing up in a mining town in Pennsylvania just after the turn of the century:

> A lantern on his miner's hat would light the way through the early dawn. I stood at the window where I had a view of the mine and I could see many lights like fireflies all heading in one direction. Then I would stand near the stove to wash and dress. The stove was our only source of heat; we were warm and cold at the same time.

Again, the context that her lines discover defies the easy, overly simplified categorization of commercial imagery. "The place we shared at the stove," she writes as the poem progresses, "was warm, but cold," a metaphoric moment she compares to life itself. Margaret has captured, like good poets do, that affirmative moment in the midst of negative forces. Her prose poem is a tribute to living—even in the midst of poverty—rather than a plea for material needs.

We are a people ripe for poetry. It is in our easy grasp to take corporate language one step further. Twist the cliché, challenge the easy sentiment, take the thought inward, trust the image, the vehicle of the imagination, which has at its core all our inexpressible dreams and fears. Extend the intuitive moment until you find the context that can serve as a home for those wandering human needs. The language of literature is teetering on the tightrope between abandon on one side and rediscovery on the other.

Sit down at the table. Place the blank sheet in front of you as if it were nothing more than a place mat upon which you could doodle or fancify your initials. Try to clear your mind so only a few thousand thoughts are evident. There's a song barely audible in the background. Listen for it as it grows from faint to familiar. Listen . . . you know it. Forget yourself until you begin to see yourself. You too, I say to myself, sipping my coffee, staring into my notebook, are on a journey—like your students. I know I must find myself somewhere—in a field, on a bridge, in a strange room, on a stairway—a place where the other self can linger in a world of imagination. I watch my pen move across the page . . . *the creak of a stair* I have written, and for a moment I feel the weight of the body in my foot. It is obvious, I say to myself, that there are two of us present, the inarticulate journeyman who must respond to the lyrical persuasions of experience, and the isolated writer who must record it all. The pen begins to move with an ease and grace I can only imagine. For a moment I can't recall where I am, in the streets where surely I will disappear, or at the table where I will find myself. I write my way across the night. In this poem, it is clear now, the two of us will meet. All that talk, I chide myself, about the relationship between poetry, people, and the community—the inspiration of this book. And yet each poem I write is a memo I attach to my life: down deep, where the poem begins, and even deeper where it ends, it is a private encounter.

The Visitor

It is
as if I were always
on my way home,
moving from the fallen beams
of black shadow
to the eerie light of hidden moon.
It is
always late enough to confuse
the issues of rest
and companionship.
It is
the last sound
of the stair that creaks
through the collective dream
of chance loves . . .

Stay awhile
says the darkness, as does
the light. *Stay awhile*
says the stone, and even
the river says it, adding it will
be back in a hundred years.
Stay awhile says the lovely;
Stay awhile says the old.
I take off my shoes
and soak in gravity's light.
I try once more
to lie back and trust my stare
to ceiling, skylight,
star . . .
Stay awhile, says the dream,
its anonymity assured.
Stay awhile says the voice
rising from the buried bone

up through the hollow
of the illuminating spine . . .

I turn around, my face
exposed to a thousand failed portraits
in the unoccupied gallery
of the wind.
I would not know the place
where I could die without considering
the distance the remains
would have to be sent.
The night falls like flesh
against a path of white linen,
which I follow, mere feet of dust,
to a window, where, under
the solitary lamp above the desk,
his head in his arms, a man sleeps . . .
While I, common wanderer,
assume his dream;
while we, collectively,
live out our lives.

DEPARTURE

*W*hen I pulled up to the baseball field on my Triumph 500 motorcycle, the green-and-white tank sparkling under the cool Wisconsin sunlight, my well-worn Gil McDougal fielder's glove strapped to the seat with a bungee cord, I could feel the absolute hatred of the fraternity boys as they warmed up, the TKE T-shirts proclaiming their bawdy identity, as they realized that the best shortstop in the league, who played on the worst team in the league (the English department), the radical commie, East Coast poet-columnist of the college newspaper, had arrived.

I loved it. Even now, twenty years later, as I remember pushing the kickstand down behind the bench and running out to the diamond smacking my little fist into the leather of my magic glove, I love it still.

In the late sixties, with the issues of the Vietnam war and civil rights so immediate in the minds and lives of college students, young people had a chance to apply ideas to real-world events. That being the basis of perspective, many of us discovered for the first time not just a point of view, but a point of view to which we could commit ourselves passionately.

My views were well-known. I had a column in the school newspaper. It became a focal point for the controversies that were energizing campuses throughout the country. One night, sipping a beer at a bar near the university, a bar that was a hangout for students and professors, I noticed a couple of fraternity boys going out of their way to bump into me.

I had been there at the bar because we gathered there almost nightly—not just my student friends and me, but professors too: an art professor whose name I can't recall; Bill, the sociology professor from Brooklyn; George, the English professor who ran the literary magazine; Dave from history; and Phil Gallo, the mysterious poet straight from the writers workshop at Iowa. Thinking back now, I am amazed at the fact that despite twenty-cent drafts, we would never get drunk. We gathered there to talk—the ideas of the classroom suddenly applied to life through our lengthy, friendly but passionate discussions, just sipping our beers, not chugging them.

It must have seemed like a conspiracy to the frat boys, and to the Veterans Club students as well. Routinely I would get pushed, beer spilled on me, four-letter words thrown my way. I had a system. I'd avoid a fight if I could, making my way to my group of friends. But I'd pick out someone from the hostile fraternity group—someone my size I could handle in a fight if I had to—and I'd confront that person in the union or cafeteria the next day. These guys, I discovered, were lost without their alcohol and their boisterous companions. One on one they were intimidated. I assumed too it was because they did not have the strength of convictions. Prejudice, which seemed to drive these guys, does not seem to create inner strength.

"What was it you wanted to say to me at the bar last night?" I said to "Hawk," one of the frat brothers who had purposely bumped into me at the bar the previous evening. He murmured something, holding his lunch tray *against him like a shield, looking nervously over his shoulder for fraternity support. He then moved on, looking for a table of comrades and turning red as I tried to look him square in the eyes.*

One night, early in the evening, I was alone at the Poodle Lounge, sitting at the end of the bar, waiting for Leo and George, two of my professors, and for Paul and Jim, two of my classmates and friends. There was hardly anyone in the bar when six or seven Veterans Club members came in and sat down at the bar next to me.

I tried to remain anonymous, but it was no use. They spotted me immediately. These guys were older, of course—all good-sized men. I might as well have been a North Vietnamese sitting there, suspected of hiding a hand grenade under my shirt, right next to the communist manifesto tucked under my belt!

One guy—the president of the Vets Club, whom I would get to know over the following months—walked down the bar until he was standing right behind me, his face no more than six inches from my ear when he whispered, with a voice filled with hatred, those three little words: "You fucking asshole!"

I don't know how I got out of that bar that night without my bones being broken. But each subsequent encounter, and there were many, reminded me of what I had come to college to learn: the power of the word. *I wasn't flashy, weird-looking, provocative, or nasty. But I had managed to write effectively. I had managed to bring thoughts to life in a sensual, imagistic manner. And although my columns were, naturally, prose, I was developing the poetics of both mind and language. The theory of the classroom was filtering its way down to the streetside confrontation. The physical threat, conveyed in that guy's own sense of poetics, was simply the embodiment of a passionate commitment to an ideal—philosophical, aesthetic, political.*

What more could I ask for as a poet? Words that drive men to action. Good friends and good enemies—that was the recipe in the sixties if we were going to confront the malaise of the middle class, the center-of-the-road politics that would leave most Americans without identifiable convictions, without—in poet Lucille Clifton's words—"a passionate commitment to something."

As I walked to school one day, one beautiful crisp sunny northern Wisconsin day, I struck up a conversation with a lovely blond coed, probably of Norwegian descent with her upturned nose, broad cheekbones, and sparkling blue eyes. By the ten minutes or so it took to get to the campus, we discovered some common interests—skiing, motorcycles, ice cream sodas at Bridgeman's Dairy. But we also discovered an attraction to each other as well. At the steps of Old Main, about to make our way to our classes, we exchanged names.

"You," she replied, taking a longer, deeper look into my eyes, reacting suddenly like someone who had been deceived into pleasantries, "You are Ross Talarico!"

She never spoke to me again, although our eyes met here and there on several occasions. Apparently my reputation was more powerful than any charm I possessed. In her mind, I was probably a lefto, pinko betrayer of the Constitution.

There were others too who thought of me as, if not a communist, at least a future communist of America. One afternoon I received a note asking if I could attend a meeting one night. It was a cordial note, and its understated tone made me curious, especially since it was not clear at all what this meeting was about and why I was being asked to attend. But on a cold spring evening, early enough for the turn-of-the-century side streets in Superior to be nearly empty, I found the alley described in the note. I knocked on the anonymous doorway and someone inside pushed aside a curtain, peeked out at me, and opened the door.

There were about ten people inside the small room, which contained some chairs and tables, a large map, a pile of notebooks, and a coffee pot. Everyone was older, in their sixties, I had guessed, and moved slowly and deliberately, each shaking my hand and whispering their admiration for the columns I had published in the college newspaper.

I don't remember much about that meeting—the first and last communist party meeting I would ever attend. They pointed at the large map with a pointer, discussing the whereabouts of other groups they were in touch with. They made a formal round of statements about conditions in America, and welcomed me to a universal group of people committed to human rights and social equality. As a young writer, I was told, I had the opportunity to spread the good word.

When I met with George Gott and Phil Gallo, the two poets—the two friends I studied under at Wisconsin . . . when I met with them for one last cup of coffee on the last day of my student life in Wisconsin, we exchanged poems, regards, and I walked back to my apartment with tears in my eyes. I knew even then how rare such friendships would be in this big, busy country where jingles, ads, and the growing persuasions of marketing executives would eliminate the dialogue between people trying to explore the soul. I put on my rain suit, tucked my diploma away, packed up my Triumph motorcycle, and took off on a twelve-hundred-mile journey back to upstate New York, where some vague notion of a poet's life awaited me.

The rain followed me east through northern Wisconsin, through Ashland and Ironwood, down the incredibly straight highways and into north-

ern Michigan. My own sentimental tears of departure had long since dried and my entire body seemed soaked with determination as the motorcycle engine pumped steady through the twilight rain. At the small town of Iron Mountain I looked for a motel to spend the night, hoping of course for a clear morning to continue my journey home. I was tired and wet, and dismayed to find that neither of the two motels took credit cards—which I had to use since I had only fifty bucks or so to make it home. So I got back on the highway as darkness fell and pressed on to Escanaba, Michigan, where surely I could find a place to sleep.

It was still raining, and my back and shoulders ached from the constant pressure of my arms on the handlebars, trying to fight the slickness of the pavement and keeping up the speed to get to Escanaba as soon as I could. In my rearview mirror I saw headlights approaching. The car passed me, but then slowed down until it was next to me, and I saw three young men in the front seat drinking from a bottle and pointing at me. Then one of them rolled down the window of the dark '57 Chevy and tossed the empty bottle at me. It glanced off my helmet and smashed on the road.

I slowed down immediately and they sped away laughing. But they were not finished. I saw them pull to the side of the pine-lined highway. I slowed again and pulled to the side of the road—I did not want to pass them and give them another shot at me. I made a U-turn on the highway and started back the other way. They quickly turned their car around and began to chase me.

I remember a talk with George and Phil at a table in the college union late in the afternoon as we exchanged new poems. I had written a line that they liked, though the poem it was a part of fell into the "promise" rather than "accomplished" category—the way of the world perhaps for a twenty-

two-year-old writer in love with ideas as well as language. The line was only the vulnerable survive . . .

The discussion that afternoon as we sat in the empty union, three men believing in the power of a precise and yet encompassing phrase, focused on the sensibility of an artist. They liked my line about vulnerability *because they knew there was something more to teach a young poet than technique. They knew they had to encourage me to open myself up to the world around me. Adventure would lead to insight, and the urge to share that insight would lead to an incredible respect for language. Phil expounded on my spontaneous line: "Yes, it's the vulnerable who survive because only those who avail themselves to penetrating emotions are capable of meaningful change."*

I thought I understood that afternoon—and I knew already I would try to live a life of adventure, risk, and fulfillment. I knew, like all good students of art, that the source of any literature I might create was the wound I would hold to the light. But speeding down an abandoned highway on a motorcycle on a rainy night in upper Michigan chased by three drunk men trying to run me down with their car, the metaphor was suddenly overwhelming. I was vulnerable, all right—but did I have to put my life on the line in order to enjoy myself?

I found a house with a light on in the middle of nowhere. I pulled in and rang the doorbell, expecting perhaps that anyone seeing a man in a helmet and donned in a rubber rain suit might come to the door with a shotgun. But some old guy heard me out, called the sheriff, and even gave me a cup of coffee. The sheriff followed me halfway to Escanaba that night, flashing his lights before he turned back to that lonely stretch of Michigan Route 2. I found a motel, took a hot shower, and had a couple of beers at the motel bar. Next to me, a traveling insurance salesman listened to my story. Finding it the perfect complement to his existence, he insisted I put a policy brochure in my pocket before I left.

The rest of the trip the next day was not uneventful. The weather cleared as I drove across the five-mile bridge at the Mackinac Peninsula into lower Michigan. But in Canada later that afternoon as I took a shortcut to upstate New York, on a small twisty road near Hamilton, the motorcycle blew a piston—and I sat on a lawn while waiting four hours for June's father's pickup truck to arrive to carry me and my Triumph bike back to Rochester.

I opened my notebook and let the pen flow: the twin hearts of the Triumph's cylinders bursting with joy and anguish . . . *I bought a cigar to celebrate something I could not yet fathom, and I held the red tip to my diploma and watched the smoke disappear into the cool green Canadian wind. And later, sitting with my motorcycle in the back of the pickup truck, I had to laugh a little at myself. No, this was not the image I had planned on: the motorcycle busted, my back aching as I leaned back against the cab of the pickup, my notebook filled with half-written inspirations.*

Yes, I laughed, feeling helpless and at the mercy of others, taking a quick glance at the incredibly blue sky as we made the last turn into my home-town here I was, about as much on my own as I'd ever be, surviving as a poet in America.

It is a warm August night at Manhattan Square Park in downtown Rochester. Little by little the curved cement steps fill up with people as the stage crew adjusts the lights, speakers, and microphones on the stage in front of the waterfalls. It is obvious that the audience will be a varied one—many black youths here to see *Vicious Crew*, the young group that won the rap competition sponsored by the city's creative writing program; senior citizens here to listen to a reading of the oral history transcriptions (poetry) that have appeared in the Sunday magazines and editorial pages of both Gannett newspapers; the hard-to-define group of middle-class patrons of literary events, here to listen to the poetry of Etheridge Knight as well as that of the city's writer-in-residence (mel).

But that's not all. There are others. A number of policemen—including off-duty officers—are here, not to protect the crowd, but to hear their police chief read his story about his delinquent behavior as a child, a story (part of our oral history transcription program) that was published in the newspaper and read by thousands of people in the Rochester area.

As a matter of fact, the juxtaposition of the authors reading this night—ex-convict Etheridge Knight, who has made a name for himself as a black poet, and white police chief Gordon Urlacher—is all too much for the newspapers to pass up. One of them, *The Times-Union,* headlines its feature with big letters: WHEN WORDS COLLIDE. They begin the article like this:

> "What happens when an ex-con exchanges words with the police chief?"

And then there is more to dramatize:

> "What to expect when a City Council member (another of the evening's authors) trades speeches with a rap group that calls itself *The Vicious Crew?*

> "Rochester will find out tomorrow, when this *unlikely cast* (my emphasis) kicks off a two-day literary festival sponsored by the City's Creative Writing Program."

The term *unlikely cast* brings a little smile to my face—because in it I see my message, the thrust of the program's purpose, is coming through. There is *nothing*, of course, unlikely about this cast. The rap group wants to say something, harmonious, with a beat and with their own words to a wider audience. The city councilwoman, reading her short story about defending her deaf father in court, wants people to see her human side—so she writes a vignette (published in our newspapers' editorial pages as well as in our community collection) instead of a speech. The police chief takes the time and trouble to tell his story not for professional reasons, but because there is something deeper, something strictly personal that he needs to share for his own sake. The black poet Knight will read his prison poems, because he knows that every experience can identify the universal thoughts and feelings in all of us.

And so the night proceeds. The ex-con and police chief enjoy each other, and the audience—different ages, backgrounds, and races—responds to them both. The older crowd falls in love with the young rappers. And for a moment, the city councilwoman sheds the dense, vague, political chatter and touches the crowd with her sensitive story. She too has donned the indirect language of literature—recreating a moment before making judgments about its meaning. All these people are opening themselves, allowing a glimpse into the experiences that define them. Ironically, the newspaper tried to sensationalize the event by doing what this country's journalistic style requires: pointing out the differences between individuals and, thus, creating barriers of distraction. Those attending the event go one vital step further: they explore those "differences" in such a nonexploitative manner that they reveal more of the core of existence—which is universal in nature—and bring people closer together.

I am deeply taken, in fact, by the closeness of everyone this night. Each group in the audience—the young blacks, the senior citizens, the yuppies, and others seem to have found the common ground. Their encouragement of each other, their appreciation, their understanding seems to provide the proper answer to those provocative questions posed by the newspaper: *what's to happen when this unlikely cast exchanges words with each other?* Well . . . if by "words" one means language and creative expression in the form of a literary experience, then "what happens" is that *people begin to identify with others—and become more gracious toward one another.*

That, sadly, is the forgotten power of language in this country: *it illuminates, and heals.*

THINKING BACK
Rosie Mitchell

There is one heaven
and one hell.
There was also one bus,
back in 1921, there in
Tuskegee, Alabama, that went
from town to town,
including Birmingham, where
I had to go to visit my cousin Francis
who was sick in a hospital there.

When you gave the driver your ticket,
you just made your way
to the back of the bus, no one
making a fuss,

just glad to be going where
you had to go.
My mom would make that same trip
on the bus when I was a baby,
and in the bus station,
waitin' in the colored section,

she'd say my name,
repeat it, *Rosie, Rosie,*
like a song that echoed through
the divider, and entered the space
where the white people sat,

and I remember she said
I was the *Rose of Sharon,* the first
blossom of spring, wild
and beautiful, the reddish-orange
as bright as a light, fresh flower itself,
fragrant and full of love . . .

And on the bus, lucky to get
a seat in the back,
I was the Rose of Sharon,
and we made our way to
our destination, all the way, over
the gravel, past the cotton
and the corn, watchin' my people
choppin' and pickin'
as we made our way, together,
blacks and whites, knowing
there is one heaven and one hell.

*Ross Talarico's poetry has been widely published in more than
200 journals and magazines, among them* The Atlantic, Poetry,
American Poetry Review, The Iowa Review, The Nation,
Shenandoah, Prairie Schooner, The North America Review, *and*
Poetry Northwest. *His essays have also appeared in a variety of
publications, from* Cultural Critique *to the editorial pages of Gannett
newspapers and the* Chicago Tribune. *He has published several
books, including* All Things as They Are: Recollections of the Sixties
(and Beyond), *prose and poetry, which was given the Lillian Fairchild
Award by the University of Rochester in 1989. His book of narrative
poetry based on the oral histories of elderly Americans,* Hearts and
Times: The Literature of Memory, *was adapted for the stage in 1994
with original music and lyrics. Talarico has lectured and read at
universities, schools, museums, community centers, and government
offices throughout the country. For almost a decade he was America's
only full-time writer-in-residence for an entire metropolitan area,
Rochester, New York. He is currently Professor of Writing and Communications at National University in San Diego, where he is director
of a unique writing program for students in all areas of study.*

Library of Congress Cataloging-in-Publication Data
Talarico, Ross, 1945–
Spreading the word : poetry and the survival of community in
America / Ross Talarico.
ISBN 0-8223-1562-9. — ISBN 0-8223-1589-0 (pbk.)
1. Talarico, Ross, 1945–   —Authorship. 2. Creative writing—
Study and teaching—New York (State)—Rochester. 3. Community
life—New York (State)—Rochester. 4. Literature and society—
United States. 5. Poetry—Social aspects—United States.
6. Rochester (N.Y.)—Intellectual life. 7. Poetry—Authorship.
I. Title.
PS3570.A34Z475   1995
808'.042'07074789—dc20   94-36497 CIP